Becoming a Teaching Assistant

Becoming a Teaching Assistant

A guide for Teaching Assistants and those working with them

Pat Drake, Angela Jacklin,
Carol Robinson and Jo Thorp

P·C·P
Paul Chapman
Publishing

Paul Chapman Publishing
A SAGE Publications Company
6 Bonhill Street, London EC2A 4PU

SAGE Publications Inc
2455 Teller Road
Thousand Oaks, California 91320

SAGE Publications India Pvt Ltd
B-42 Panchsheel Enclave
Post Box 4109
New Delhi 100 017

Library of Congress Control Number available 2003106697

A catalogue record for this book is
available from the British Library

ISBN 0 7619 4356 0
ISBN 0 7619 4357 9 (pbk)

Typeset by TW Typesetting, Plymouth, Devon
Printed in Great Britain by
TJ International Ltd, Padstow, Cornwall

Contents

Acknowledgements

There are a number of individuals and organisations who contributed in many ways to the development of this book. First and foremost we would like to thank the teaching assistants, without whom this book would not have been possible. In particular, our thanks go to Chris Cooper, Ann Dann, Jane Johnstone and Beverley Linnett, as well as the students from the 2001–2 and 2002–3 cohorts of the Diploma in Professional Education Studies at the University of Sussex who participated in interviews, trialled materials and read draft chapters. We are extremely grateful to them all for their enthusiasm, support and tolerance. We would also like to extend our thanks to colleagues at the University of Sussex Institute of Education, especially Michael Eraut, Harry Torrance, Simon Thompson and Lori Altendorff for their critical comments and helpful suggestions.

The research and development phases on which this book was based depended on support from East Sussex, West Sussex and Brighton and Hove local education authorities, a grant from the University of Sussex Teaching and Learning Development Fund (2002–3) and a DfES-funded project (Barriers to QTS for Teaching Assistants, 2002). We are grateful to them all for their support.

Lastly, we would like to extend special thanks to Maddy Robbins, who coped magnificently with both us and the manuscript. Thank you Maddy.

Introduction

If you have picked up this book you are probably either a teaching assistant about to embark on further development or training, or a teacher or a lecturer helping to support teaching assistants through further education or training. The fact that you are taking this step is as a result of a huge sea change in the acknowledgement of the place of teaching assistants in schools, and recognition of the important part they can play in supporting the teaching and learning of pupils. For the first time in our history of education, career development for teaching assistants is coming to be seen as an essential aspect of making the most of schooling for young people.

Some teaching assistants are nurturing ambitions to progress in career terms eventually to become teachers. Others may be interested more in developing distinct aspects of their work to support teaching and learning collegially alongside teachers. Whether aiming to qualify as teachers or as higher-level teaching assistants or simply seeking professional development, increasingly, teaching assistants are turning to universities and colleges for programmes of professional development. For some it is the first time that they have set foot in this environment.

WHY WRITE THIS BOOK?

Following requests from the local education authorities in our region we have been working with secondary teaching assistants at undergraduate level. This has been very exciting but during this time it became clear that there were no books or resources that really addressed the situation our students faced: entering higher education for the first time as mature students on a day-release basis, and relating their study at university to their working practices at school. Teaching assistants are taking on more and more responsibility and working in larger numbers in a wider range of classes than ever before, and as a result are developing their own education theories and organisational structures. Coming together in a higher-education setting encourages the articulation of those theories, or an exchange of ideas, comparison of school structures, reflection on practice, and increasing confidence in, and consciousness of, the signifi-cance of the work that they do in schools.

A grant from the DfES enabled research into barriers that teaching assistants faced if they aimed to become qualified teachers. As well as a survey of local provision, we interviewed a range of teaching assistants and carried out case studies to investigate the nature of their work, and thoughts about career progression. It became apparent that where training courses did exist, they tended to be self-contained and unconnected to other courses. Thus, teaching assistants, however enthusiastic, tended not to be able to access a coherent path of further development tailored to their needs. What also became clear from this project was the range of roles undertaken by teaching assistants, from teacher-like work to ancil-lary-type activities. The relationships between teaching assistants and teachers are subtle and complex, and through the project we were able to discern some of the factors that make those relationships mutually successful and fulfilling.

A further grant from the University of Sussex Teaching and Learning Development Fund enabled us to bring together the findings of our earlier research with our work with mature students in higher education. The research projects informed our teaching and our learning, just as our teaching, our mutual learning and the experiences of the teaching assistants at work informed the direction of the research. This book, reflecting this complementarity, is a means of disseminating the shared experience of working as teachers, researchers and students together, in a manner that will equally support others setting out on a similar journey of exploration and development. The stories of the teaching assistants are included as a means of raising significant issues about relating learning to work, from their perspective. Each chapter includes activities for readers to do, to help make explicit their own thoughts, feelings, ideas and theories.

The teaching assistants we worked with were mainly, although not exclusively, women. Not surprisingly, the stories therefore reflect the position and status of women in low-paid occupations, struggling to combine work in school with work to sustain family and friends. Taking on the additional challenge of entering higher education added pressure to already full lives, and this pressure is evident in several of the stories that are included. Readers may also want to engage with the issues that this dimension raises.

WHO IS THE BOOK FOR?

This book is intended mainly for teaching assistants enrolled on higher-education programmes in England and Wales, and aims to facilitate transition into undergraduate study. As such it is essentially introductory in nature. Sections I and II would be of interest to any teaching assistants entering higher education. In Sections III and IV there is some reference to the National Curriculum for England and for Wales and to the developments for teaching assistants led by the Teacher Training Agency (TTA). The text will be a useful teaching resource for tutors in higher education. It will also provide the line managers of teaching assistants in schools with in-school support for professional development. The book offers professional training with respect to teaching assistants' work in schools, and a step in progression toward qualified teacher status or higher-level teaching assistant status for those who want it.

HOW IS THE BOOK ORGANISED?

The book is arranged in four sections: Experiences of entering higher education; Learning in higher education; Developing professional skills and knowledge; Issues of professionalism. We do not expect that the book will be read as a single narrative (although we hope that readers would enjoy doing so should they wish). Rather, students, mentors, tutors and line managers will be able to draw on and use sections that are immediately pertinent to arising needs. An expanded contents page should help navigate for this purpose. Throughout the book we have used the word 'pupils' to indicate school students, so as to differentiate from 'students', which is used to indicate university or college students.

Each section is introduced by a short preface highlighting the main issues raised in the chapters, so that readers can dip in and out of the material just as easily as following a continuous narrative. Course tutors will therefore be able to use the material in any order, according to preference and course structure. In terms of structure and style, the book develops from providing direct guidance in Sections I and II, to becoming more analytical and critical in Sections III and IV, so as to provide exemplification of what this means for students new to higher education. Each chapter is punctuated by activities for teaching assistants to think about, discuss, or research, thereby creating a continuous link between work experience and school practice, and development as learners.

Section I: Experiences of entering higher education. In this section experiences of others who have faced the challenges of studying in higher education are presented, from first steps towards choosing a suitable course, through to dealing with challenges arising out of acquiring funding, and from balancing work, family life and study. The section provides the means to engage with issues through four case studies of teaching assistants, supplemented by other examples. It leads towards consideration of the gains to be made professionally by combining work with study, which, in the cases highlighted, offsets the sacrifices made.

Section II: Learning in higher education. This section offers a practical guide to studying in higher education, and deals specifically with a range of study skills. The section focuses on what it means to study, and offers practical support and strategies in understanding what will be expected of you.

Section III: Developing professional skills and knowledge. In this section we examine three issues that impinge significantly on the work of teaching assistants in schools: implementing national strategies, inclusion and behaviour management. Teaching assistants, in order to expand their remit in schools, will want to understand some of the thinking underpinning these issues, and to be ready to make sense of them in their own school settings.

Section IV: Issues of professionalism. Expectations of the contribution of teaching assistants are increasing, as are the expectations from teaching assistants for recognition and status. Routes to teacher accreditation have become more abundant. A growing sense of professionalism is emerging, and in this section of the book we discuss how and why this has happened, and what it might mean for teaching assistants.

Pat Drake, Angela Jacklin, Carol Robinson and Jo Thorp
University of Sussex

Experiences of entering higher education

Chapter 1: I never thought I'd be here, but here I am

This chapter provides case studies of teaching assistants entering higher education, focusing on how students arrive at college or university, and their feelings at confronting study at an undergraduate level. Through the case studies you will evaluate motivations, apprehensions and your prior experiences, including your work as a teaching assistant in schools.

Chapter 2: Preparing for your course

By considering some of the initial experiences of other teaching assistants in their early steps in higher education, strategies are conveyed that you may employ in confronting your own challenges. For example, how did students persuade school managers to agree to day-release to attend a course? Or, how have students arranged funding for their studies?

Chapter 3: Developing as a learner

In this chapter you address explicitly some of the issues students face as they begin the process of studying in higher education. For example, ways that students balance their family lives with studying; how work in school can be balanced with work at university; gaining a clear picture of the requirements and outcomes of the course or programme itself.

Chapter 4: Succeeding and growing in confidence

This chapter highlights the positive gains that teaching assistants have made while combining work in school with study, drawing again on case studies to show both the application of theory in the work setting, and the development of skills as learners in a university. In this chapter you will revisit some of the barriers individuals described in Chapters 2 and 3 and consider how they have been addressed.

I never thought I'd be here, but here I am

You are probably entering or deciding whether to enter higher education, possibly for the first time. This can be a large step, and sometimes a decision that requires courage. The aim of this chapter is to enable you to look at your position on starting a course, and to highlight some of the experiences you will bring to your studies that provide a good starting point from which to be successful. You may never have thought you'd be here, but you may also be surprised at the potential you already have.

The chapter goes on to look at some of the worries that other teaching assistants have had on entering college or university and the motivations that have helped them to overcome these anxieties. It will remind you that although taking on undergraduate study may be a challenge, it is one you are confronting for particular reasons. In the final section you are prompted to question the course you have chosen.

The main issues raised in this chapter are as follows:

- **Thinking about experiences you bring to training**. How past experiences will be valuable in choosing to start an undergraduate course, and in developing your role as a teaching assistant.

- **Personal worries**. Understanding apprehensions that you, and others starting the course with you, will have about studying.

- **Motivation overcomes apprehension**. Examining your motivations in starting out in higher education, and how these may help you overcome apprehensions.

- **Extending your learning**. Starting to understand yourself as a learner, and aligning your own dispositions in learning with the course you have chosen.

THINKING ABOUT EXPERIENCES YOU BRING TO TRAINING

Janet has been a teaching assistant at the same school for four years. She decided to become a teaching assistant after her two children reached secondary school age. She heard the job was available and decided to apply for it as the work was convenient and fitted in with looking after her children.

> I already fancied a change from working with the young adults and decided that it would be nice to get an inside view of the school, and it meant I could still be around for the children when they came home from school and during the school holidays.

The job was not only convenient as it meant she was able to look after her children, it also offered an extension to her most recent work experience, as she had been working with young adults in a home for youngsters with learning difficulties. Before Janet had children she had worked for an electricity company, in their customer services department, and in a large bank, eventually becoming a head cashier.

When working as a teaching assistant, Janet reached a stage where she felt that she would like more from her job. To move on from this position, Janet decided that she wanted to become a teacher, and that she would like to start a course that would allow her to qualify as a teacher. This was not a step that she had imagined herself taking when she first became a teaching assistant. She felt that she had developed the confidence to become a teacher specifically through her work.

> When I first started the job I hadn't thought about becoming a teacher; in fact it was the opposite, I thought I'd never be able to stand in front of a class or control a class, I thought what a difficult job they had, but after a couple of years I began to think 'I could do that' and I became bored with the work I was doing, I wanted more . . . I started looking for something else to do about 18 months before this course came about as I felt I needed more.

This was how Janet came to decide that she would enrol in higher education. Janet's story raises several points.

- Janet had gained valuable experiences before starting her course that would help her indirectly both in studying and in trying to become a teacher, even though this experience was not in school. Both her work with the electricity company and bank involved dealing with people face to face, which gave her the confidence and skills to help her communicate ideas to the pupils she currently supports.

- Through related professional experiences (in her work with young adults), Janet gained the confidence to apply for a job as a teaching assistant.

- Finally, Janet described how, through her work as a teaching assistant, her confidence had grown to a point where she felt able to train as a teacher.

Experiences before starting your course give you practical skills and also the personal confidence to apply to your studies, both in taking on the challenge of study and in being willing to develop the way you work individually and with others.

Lisa's history of becoming a teaching assistant is similar to Janet's. Lisa worked teaching basic skills to adults before she became a teaching assistant. She feels that many of the skills she acquired through this have been put to use. Working with these adults also gave her a strong perspective on how to deal with children who struggle in lessons. 'If you've done basic skills it just gives you a different insight into things. It just gives you a whole different slant on things; you automatically pick up a worksheet and think "that's no good because they won't be able to use it".'

So, as well as experiences offering skills that are indirectly related to developing as a teaching assistant, you may also have skills that are directly transferable, such as Lisa's previous teaching experience. These will not only allow you to 'better' approach challenges you will meet in training, they will also provide some of the basis for your individual understanding of how you might develop professionally.

▶ ACTIVITY 1.1

Think about your experiences and jot down your response to the following questions:

- What professional experiences do you have that may be valuable in your work as a teaching assistant and in higher education? Think about the general skills required of you in previous jobs you have held; for example, time-management skills or administrative skills.

- As well as working as a teaching assistant, what experiences do you have of working with people trying to learn? And, how do you think you apply these skills to your work as a teaching assistant?
- Janet had to develop her confidence in her work in order to feel that she could apply for an undergraduate course. Can you think of any areas in which you have developed your own confidence, and which you think will help you on the course you are starting out on?

Janet's story is important in so far as you will also have experiences that will be valuable in developing your practice and understanding of the learning process in schools. The challenge is to recognise these experiences and allow them to contribute to your process of learning. Other teaching assistants we spoke to had an equally wide range of experiences, incorporating many valuable skills, including their experiences as parents.

PERSONAL WORRIES

Despite Janet having developed confidence, she still had some apprehensions about starting the course.

> I was apprehensive before I started, basically mainly because it had been a lot of years since I'd done any sort of academic work. It's one thing helping kids with their work, but it's another actually learning to be a teacher, and never having been to university, I didn't know what sort of level the work was going to be. I didn't know what to expect the other people to be like. Going to uni seemed such a huge step. I was also worried about how I was going to fit it all in, I just didn't know until I'd started, it's been a really hard year, but I've thoroughly enjoyed it. All my family knew I really wanted to do it, but I don't think they realised how difficult it was to fit everything in.

We can see that Janet was worried about several things. Some of her concerns may be issues for you too. It may be useful to draw some of these out.

1. *A long break from study:* For Janet, going back to university was a challenge as she had been out of education for a long period of time. She was taking the step into higher education and she was also starting out on a transformation in her career. Naturally she felt worried as she was

uncertain about what would be asked of her. For Janet, going to university would be both an academic challenge and a big personal step.

2. *Meeting others:* Janet was unsure about meeting new people in an unfamiliar environment.

3. *Finding the time:* Janet was worried about fitting in the other elements of her life alongside the course. Clearly her family were an important part of this anxiety for her. Today we tend to work longer and longer hours, and fitting everything in can seem very daunting. The management of time and such practical issues is very important and will be dealt with in detail in Chapter 3.

▶ ACTIVITY 1.2

It is helpful to start by identifying your hopes and concerns. Often you will find you are not alone and others are experiencing similar feelings. Think about the next question and jot down your thoughts:

■ What worries you about starting out at university? Like Janet you may be worried about dealing with the workload, or you may be worried about more personal issues, such as getting on with others.

Here are some examples of what other teaching assistants have told us about the feelings they experienced when entering higher education:

Amanda: I was worried about what would be expected of me intellectually, and whether I would be able to live up to it ... There's an awful lot of people investing things in you and there's a certain amount of pressure.

Pam: I'm not bragging but I knew I could do it because I'd done the Open University course. It was more to do with time – would I have time to do everything?

Alison: I was apprehensive about my age; I'm 50. I was worried that I'd be the oldest member of the course.

What these points tell us is that everybody will have both hopes and worries when starting out on a course. Some of these will be the same as other people's and other hopes and concerns will be quite individual. For example, as Pam had been on an Open University course she was not worried about the level of writing that would be expected. However, she did have other concerns. Your past experiences will be important in defining what hopes and apprehensions you have. You may find it helpful to start by acknowledging them and remembering that you are not alone.

MOTIVATION OVERCOMES APPREHENSION

Despite their initial worries, Janet, and the other teaching assistants whose experiences are featured in this book, made their way into higher education. If you are reading this, the chances are that you have gone through a similar process.

▶ ACTIVITY 1.3

About your motivation:

- What motivated you to decide to start a course at a university or higher-education institution? It is very important to remind yourself of the initial reasons you set out to achieve a qualification, as this will help you to meet the challenges throughout your course.

We have already seen that Janet was bored with her work, and that she was looking to move on to something new. She described how she jumped at an opportunity she had been waiting for.

> I started looking for something else to do about 18 months before this course came about, as I felt I needed more. I'd tried every avenue I could, and I found my only option, if I wanted to do a higher education course or to become a teacher, was to stop work and do a course full-time, but that wasn't possible for me as my husband had been made redundant twice and we couldn't afford for me to give up work, so I continued working and just sat tight and waited for something to come along. When I saw the course details I couldn't believe it, I had to look at them a few times, it was exactly what I'd been looking for, I could hardly believe what I was reading!

Janet had specific ends in mind before she started her studies, and so when the right course came along it was a chance to fulfil her ambition. While she had been motivated to go into training for some time, she was frustrated by the lack of opportunity.

Lisa identified different reasons for being motivated to start studying in higher education.

> A letter came from the Education Action Zone and that was it. It was really weird because I thought: 'Oh I think I'll do this', because I'd just finished

my City and Guilds 7307 the previous year and I thought 'well, I'm in a
learning mood'. I had wanted to go on to study further and then the details
of the course came through and I thought 'I'll have a go at that'.

Lisa's reasons for wanting to start a course are quite different to those of
Janet's. She enjoyed the previous courses she had been on and was
looking for a way to develop her training. The university course enabled
her to do this. Lisa's motivation for entering higher education demonstrates that there are those who enjoy learning (not entirely for its own
sake), and are looking for ways to extend their learning in a way that is
relevant to their working lives without wishing to become teachers.

EXTENDING YOUR LEARNING

Janet's comment: 'When I saw the course details I couldn't believe it, I
had to look at them a few times, it was exactly what I'd been looking for,
I could hardly believe what I was reading!' is important. It shows us that
she knew what she was looking for in a higher-education course before
the details arrived.

▶ ACTIVITY 1.4

Janet knew what she wanted from the course she started. The question below
may help you look at the course you hope to start in more detail:

- Can you list what you want from your undergraduate course?

The course will enable you to achieve certain ends. You may also find it
helpful to think about the point you are starting from. By doing this you
begin to develop a picture of yourself growing as a professional and a
learner by, for example, gaining a qualification or fulfilling a long-term
ambition. As Nicky explained:

> I just got into the habit of always doing a course every year and I kept doing
> this. There are only so many GCSEs and after I had my five I wanted
> something to do that was going to be of use in my work.

For Nicky and Lisa we can begin to see a 'career' in adult learning. They
have started doing courses and have become used to doing so over several
years. The decision to start higher education was, for both of them, a
further step in developing this career, and one that they felt was natural

for them to take. The point that these stories convey is that Nicky and Lisa reached a stage where they felt able to take on learning at a higher-education level.

▶ ACTIVITY 1.5

You have chosen a course that will allow you to achieve your aims. How are *you* matched to this course?

■ What experiences do you have that help you feel ready to take your first steps in higher education? As stated earlier, these may not simply be experiences from formal education, but also those in your work or family.

The examples in this chapter can help you evaluate important experiences you have before starting a course. We can now go on to look at first steps in preparing for higher education.

CHAPTER 2

Preparing for your course

This chapter is based on the experiences of Alison and four other teaching assistants, Pam, Janet, Amanda and Dave. Overall, the aim is to look at issues that other teaching assistants have found useful to consider before they started a course. We start by revisiting some of the issues raised in the previous chapter; then we look at areas that will be helpful for you to consider before starting out. The final section looks at the experiences of Alison and Pam as they enter higher education. In this way we aim to bring you to the door of your first seminar or lecture.

The following are some of the key issues this chapter will raise:

- **Experiences leading up to higher education**. You will be encouraged to think about past experiences that you bring to training

- **Negotiating time and funding**. This will help you to understand some of the issues you will have to arrange with the school where you work, before you start a course.

- **Life at home, life at work and your studies**. You will be encouraged to think about the challenge of balancing your studies with other commitments in your life, particularly anticipating issues before they become a problem; and understanding how other teaching assistants have met these challenges.

- **Through the door**. We will look at the shared experiences of other teaching assistants in their very first experience of entering higher education.

EXPERIENCES LEADING UP TO HIGHER EDUCATION

Alison has been a teaching assistant for six years at the same school. Her career leading up to this was varied and included raising a family. When she was a teenager, on leaving school she decided that she would like to be a teacher and enrolled on an education degree, but she did not feel able to stay on this course and so left university. She then went to work as a secretary, but still thought of becoming a teacher. She married, and in the following years Alison and her husband built up a company importing pottery from France. Alison developed the French she knew to the extent that she could conduct business with overseas contacts. However, as garden centres started to take over the market for pots, the business began to struggle. When her children were at school she was asked if she would like to work as a volunteer helper, and eventually if she would like to join the staff as a teaching assistant.

▶ ACTIVITY 2.1

With Alison's experience in mind try to answer the following question:

- What value do you think Alison's experiences may have for her learning and professional development?

Alison started by thinking about the experiences and skills she had gained:

- She had been successful enough at school to apply to a degree course. This gave her confidence that she would be able to study in higher education.

- Secretarial work gave her administrative and organisational skills.

- Through starting and developing her business she showed the ability to carry a high level of responsibility and use her initiative, communicate with others professionally, and manage time and money. In this time she developed her knowledge of French and so has shown a willingness and ability to learn new things.

- As a parent she has experience of the challenges her children faced in moving through different school age groups. She has seen the positive and negative aspects of their experiences of school, and through this has gained understanding of the experiences many other children share.

NEGOTIATING TIME AND FUNDING

Alison faced several barriers in getting onto her course. Initially, as she explains, there was the process of negotiating funding with school managers:

> The head originally said that only one member of staff from the school could attend the course, and three of us had wanted to do it. What he decided in the end was that he would pay a proportion of the fees for two of us to do the course. I paid £155 and the school paid the balance, and because I did not work on the day the course is on, I had to do it in my own time.

Because other teaching assistants in the school also wished to attend the course, in looking for the funding to study Alison had to reach a position of compromise.

The teaching assistants we interviewed in our research (Thorp *et al.*, 2002) had some widely varying experiences. At one end of the spectrum, some teaching assistants were given paid time off school to attend courses and had their fees paid. At the other end of the spectrum, some teaching assistants supported themselves and were asked to make up any time they took off school. For example, Dave faced a difficult situation because there was a lack of communication between the head teacher and a deputy.

> The deputy was supposed to sort it out, and he said 'here this course is, you can have a day a week to do it', then the head said 'no'. And so I've ended up doing stuff in break times and do an hour of homework club . . . slop duty at lunchtime.

The provision of training opportunities is new ground, and some schools are still finding their way. Perhaps an important lesson we can learn from Dave's experience is to be clear about what you will need, and what will be offered before committing to a course. Do your homework and negotiate thoughtfully with colleagues in school.

▶ ACTIVITY 2.2

These questions may help you to clarify certain issues. You may wish to talk to others about them, or confirm them for your own peace of mind.

- Are you clear of how your school might support you should you wish to start a course in higher education?
- Are there any sources, other than money held by your school, that might pay for some of your course?

Pam addressed these issues before she was able to start a higher-education course. In negotiating with senior management, and by seeking other funding, Pam placed herself in a position where she was able to start the course.

> When the head wasn't keen for me to do the course, I went to see my SEN coordinator and said that I was going to do it one way or the other, even if it meant that I would work for just four days a week. She spoke to the head who eventually agreed for me to do the course. He only agreed to fund half of the course though, rather than the 70 per cent that most schools seemed to fund.

Because of this difficult situation, Pam had to find the balance of the fees from elsewhere. However, many teaching assistants such as Janet and Amanda (below) found their schools supportive in allowing them to study in higher education.

> *Janet*: The school was fine about me doing the course, they were really pleased for me, it wasn't a problem at all. I did the course on my day off, but they paid the 70 per cent course fees for me. I was worried about whether the school would be supportive, but they've been really supportive. My SEN coordinator, in particular, is always there to help if I need her.

> *Amanda*: The SEN coordinator felt it was important that as a senior teaching assistant I had the opportunity to do the course. Everything that can be done to facilitate us doing this course has been done by the SEN coordinator and senior management. I know I'm really lucky to say that because I do know that isn't the position for some of my colleagues who have been on the course.

One source of funding that schools have available for training teaching assistants is the Standards Fund. This is a government grant that each school receives, a proportion of which is designated for the professional development of teaching assistants. If your school is unable to help you fund the course, you could contact the local education authority in which you work. Several local education authorities work in partnership with universities to provide training, and they may have some funds retained to help teaching assistants attend these courses, although much will have been devolved to schools. In light of the new proposals, however, funding arrangements are likely to change (DfES, 2002b). It will be important to check arrangements at the time of your application. It is to be hoped that in the future teaching assistants will not face the confused situations some of those we spoke to had to negotiate.

LIFE AT HOME, LIFE AT WORK AND YOUR STUDIES

Alison described difficulties in managing to fit the course around other commitments. Lizzie also experienced difficulties, partly because of the way she saw her role in the family:

> My husband didn't like it, I think because it took my time and he didn't think it would make a difference to my earning ability, but that wasn't my main reason for doing it, I was doing it for me. I did find it a bit difficult at times, and felt that I had to keep the house running because that's what I'd always done, and if I didn't do that then I think my husband would have really objected. As it was, he was not happy about me working in the evenings, but I was determined to do it.

There may be difficult personal barriers in starting out; these may be to do with people around you who may be affected by you starting your course. You may feel a strong commitment to your family, and guilt about not fulfilling expectations held of you, yet at the same time you may really want to balance these feelings against requirements made of you on the course.

Pam described how she felt that she could expect her family to give her time to complete her coursework:

> There are times when I've just had to say 'Sorry, I'm doing it for me.' I got to the stage where I thought: if things don't get done, tough! It's very difficult, but I think you just have to be determined to do it for yourself and realise that you don't have to feel guilty just because you are not running around after everyone.

This was a big step for Pam, and she felt a sense of guilt at not offering her family the time that she would have done before starting the course. However, she felt she needed this time for her studies.

Alison and others describe this adjustment as one of the most difficult aspects of their studies. Alison also describes coming through this challenge as being a significant personal achievement:

> I found my time was limited and I had to give myself limitations about how much time I spent on work. I tend to leave things until the last minute, so I had to be really strict about how much time I spent on things, but once I

decided to work I'd really go for it. I mean I passed, but I really struggled to fit it all in.

Your studies will affect the amount of time you have available for your family. Feeling comfortable with the balance between your study time and the time you would like to give to your family does present quite a challenge.

▶ ACTIVITY 2.3

Take time to consider these next three points. Again, you may find it helpful to jot down your thoughts.

- Which parts of your personal life is it important to maintain time for? How will these elements fit around your study?
- What compromises will you have to make? You will need to make time for study, so where will this time come from?
- In what ways can those around you be supportive? Your close friends or family may be affected by your studies, but they can also be a great help in this time. Are there specific ways these people can help you?

THROUGH THE DOOR
■

As you will have realised, there are lots of arrangements to make before you start your course. You need to talk to your managers at school regarding possible funding and time to study, and talk to your family about the personal commitment you will need to make to higher education. In some senses, once you have made these practical arrangements you are 'ready' to start a course.

The first step into higher education can be both exciting and daunting at the same time. Despite her wide-ranging experiences Alison still felt apprehensive about some aspects of going back to university:

> The first thing I did when I went in the room was to look around and see if there was anyone older than me, and to see the level of people on the course. I did notice that there were not many men, and I found the people there comfortingly normal. I felt at ease straight away. In the first lesson we all introduced ourselves and that was really good; it forced us to talk to each other.

This is similar to the feelings Pam felt when she started her course:

> I felt a mixture really of apprehension, but at the same time looking forward
> to it. I wondered how we were all going to get on, but everyone was so
> friendly; we all felt at ease and liked each other, we were all from the same
> background.

For both Pam and Alison their initial worries about starting out on the
course were set aside quickly once they had met the group they would
study with. This draws out a key point about the nature of studying at
higher education. Remember, you will face similar challenges and
experiences as others on the course. You will not be confronting problems
alone. Similarly, the process of learning partly rests upon learning being
a social event; people talking to, and supporting, one another. If you are
starting a course for teaching assistants you will be learning with other
teaching assistants.

REFERENCES

DfES (2002b) *Developing the Role of School Support Staff: Consultation Paper,*
London: DES: October 2002.

Thorp, J., Robinson, C., Jacklin, A. and Drake, P. (2002) *Routes into
Teaching for Teaching Assistants,* Unpublished report to the DES:
University of Sussex, July 2002.

CHAPTER 3

Developing as a learner

This chapter moves forward from your first experiences in higher education. Once you have prepared yourself to start a course, the process is one of finding your way, problem-solving, developing your own style as a learner and coming to a better understanding of how you achieve what is asked of you.

The questions you are asked to reflect on range from the very broad, aiming to develop your understanding of a 'good learner', to the quite specific, looking at issues you might face about finding resources to help you with your studies. In thinking about these questions, you should remember that the answers will be quite personal. The aim is to facilitate a clearer picture for you of how to become reflective in your studies, and hence find your own way through a course.

The following are some of the issues that this chapter will raise:

- **How Joan reached higher education**. Joan's story of how she came to reach higher education will allow you to recap on some of the issues dealt with in the previous chapters.

- **Learning in higher education as a process**. Using examples, we will look at times when Joan and other teaching assistants met challenges and overcame them. These events demonstrate their personal development, and give us ideas of some useful characteristics of successful learning.

- **Settling into your own way of working**. You will prefer to learn in certain conditions and ways. This section is an introduction to establishing your own patterns of work, and how you organise other factors to help you study in the ways that suit you.

■ **Resources and your studies**. Several of the teaching assistants you have met so far describe problems they faced with finding resources for their studies. The ways in which they coped with these challenges may help you deal with similar problems.

HOW JOAN REACHED HIGHER EDUCATION

Joan decided to become a teaching assistant after helping out at dinner duty in a school. When a position as a teaching assistant arose locally she applied for the job, encouraged to do so by the staff in the school where she was working at lunchtimes. She was pleased to find work that fitted in around her own children being at school.

She has now been a teaching assistant for three years at the same school. In this time she has attended a number of training courses, and felt that these were valuable not just for their content.

> I think they are really important, not just for what you learn on the course but because you mix with other teaching assistants and get ideas from them about how they work and how their school operates and how they deal with different situations.

She valued the experiences of teaching assistants from other schools and felt that these practical insights were useful in learning about her job. However, she also felt that she would like to take a step further in developing her work. This was not simply a professional decision; it was also related to her motivation for personal achievement.

> I was going to achieve something in my life as a mother, suddenly I was about to start doing something which was for me.

She hoped to achieve something for herself as she felt motivated and comfortable making this independent step. She describes below some of the necessary arrangements she needed to make with her school before starting out.

> The first hurdle was to get on the course, to write a letter and get accepted. Once that was sorted, the next hurdle was to persuade the school to let all three of us do the course . . . It was difficult to get the funding. We had to keep on at them, but we managed, and the school paid 70 per cent for each of us, but it meant we all had to work more than our 20 hours a week.

So, after some persuasion the school agreed to part-fund several teaching assistants to go on the course. These teaching assistants also had to compress the hours they worked into four full-time days so that they could use the spare day to attend university. Although the school was accommodating, the teaching assistants had to compromise in order to be able to go on the course. Only after this process was Joan able to reach the point where she could start her studies.

> On the very first day, we couldn't find the room, so things weren't off to a very good start! I was very nervous on the first day, but excited at the same time – it was like a new venture for me.

Joan was both hopeful and anxious!

▶ ACTIVITY 3.1

Joan's story provides a history of steps she took which led to entering university. Could you give a similar account of your own story? If you were to advise someone else, what would you tell them were the key aspects?

LEARNING IN HIGHER EDUCATION AS A PROCESS

The previous chapters have dealt with issues that we hope will be useful for you to think about before starting out on a course. However, studying in higher education will not be something you can prepare for completely, as you will have to adjust and deal with challenges as they arise. To try to illustrate this we will use two quite diverse examples of Joan's experiences: how she came to a better understanding of how to make the most of tutorials, and how she dealt with pressures of studying for a maths GCSE at the same time as studying at university. Although the situations are quite different, in both cases Joan met a challenge in her learning and worked through it.

Here, Joan describes how she learnt to make the most of tutorials:

> The problem was I didn't take enough opportunity of the tutorials, I didn't really understand what they were for, I'd get my essay to a nearly final stage and then go and see my tutor and he'd say I had to make all these alterations, whereas I'd have been better off going to see my tutor when I'd done a first draft.

As the course went on she came to understand that it would be more helpful if she went to see her tutor at an earlier point in writing her essays. It was only by going through the process of completing a piece of work that she came to an understanding of how she could use the systems of support available in a way that suited her. Through this she felt more able to improve the work she handed in for assessment. You may find that your personal preferences are different to Joan's; it is only by trying things out (and occasionally getting it wrong) that you will be able to learn what suits you.

Joan also found that there was some difficulty with a maths GCSE course she was attending:

> The maths GCSE was a modular course and it just seemed to coincide with the deadlines for the university course, so at times I was really struggling to get things finished. You had to be fairly well organised, and I'm not a great organiser, but having seen this course and decided to go for it, I just had to find a way of fitting everything in.

As she was going through the two courses; it emerged that the deadlines for work overlapped. Joan's response to dealing with this was to make sure she organised her time and to seek support with childcare. Her strong motivation, and desire to make a personal achievement gave her the energy to make such changes.

▶ ACTIVITY 3.2

Using Joan's example you might start thinking about strategies that will help you adapt to make the most of your course.

- Looking at the examples Joan gives, what are some of the strategies she has found effective in helping her to become a better learner?

Some of the answers to this question are useful lessons we can all make use of.

Joan is willing (and keen) to adapt to what is going on around her. This means being open to ideas that help her develop her strategies for learning. She explained this as follows:

> You can't be too set in your ways and you have to accept that there are different ways of doing things, so if you've always done something one way and someone comes up with a better way of doing it, then you've got to be able to accept that.

For example, she doesn't regard herself as an organised person, yet when she realised that there would be points where she would face a considerable workload, Joan decided that she had to be more efficient in organising her studies.

A second point is that she did not isolate herself when she came up against problems, but as she puts it: 'I think you've got to accept that you can't get through it on your own; you need the help of others'.

▶ ACTIVITY 3.3

Use Figure 3.1 below to list the sort of support you may need. Then, next to each type of support, note down where that support might come from.

Type of support	Who can help
Study	
Mobility	
Transport	
Child care	
Financial	

3.1 THINKING ABOUT SUPPORT

Joan shows us two key parts of being able to grow as a learner in higher education: firstly, a willingness to be *flexible* and adapt; and secondly, a willingness to *make learning a social process*, seeking the help of others both in learning itself and the support she will need around her studies.

SETTLING INTO YOUR OWN WAY OF WORKING

You will have to develop a feel for these broad issues as you start out in higher education. Below are some examples of such points from Joan.

> It sounds silly, but one of the things that helped was getting books out of the library. Every week, I used to do that, go and get books out and then I'd look through some of them at home. I kind of felt that I needed the back-up of books, and if I had that, I felt more confident about what I was doing with my university work. I need quietness to work and this can be difficult at home because you can't say to the rest of the family that they can't watch television because you want to work, so I used to work in the evenings and go into the kitchen mainly when the children were in bed.

Other teaching assistants worked in different ways:

> *Janet*: I find it best to work when everybody else is out, so the time when I worked varied from week to week, depending on what the rest of the family were doing.

> *Alison*: I found it really good to have a support network; you've then got people to turn to when you are having problems with things, and this was easy to build up because the people on the course were so friendly and we were all in the same situation.

> *Nicky*: Sally, who also works here, can pick up her books at break time and do twenty minutes of work. I can't do that. I have to clear a block of time and give myself that to concentrate. It's hard sometimes because that means I have to find times where I can do that, but I have to do it.

These are just a few examples of how, on becoming students, teaching assistants have discovered ways of working that suit them. Some of them are quite individual, like Joan feeling more comfortable if she had books out from the library; others may be true for many of us, like finding a quiet space to work in. The last quote from Nicky shows that one person's way of working will be quite different from that of another. Whereas her colleague who was also on a course could work in short bursts, this was not something Nicky was able to do. If you have these preferences you are better off allowing yourself the space to work as you wish, rather than forcing yourself to work in a way that does not come naturally. For Nicky this meant that she had to organise her time quite strictly.

▶ ACTIVITY 3.4

We can start to build a picture of Joan as a learner, using some statements that match her preferred ways of working (see Figure 3.2).

■ Can you think of a set of statements that would be true of you as a learner? Think about the ways you prefer to work normally and see if you think they might apply to your studies.

This is a useful starting point for two reasons. First, you can think of some of the ways that will be best for you before you are far into your course. Second, your learning preferences may change over time. You can return to this activity later to see in what ways this has happened.

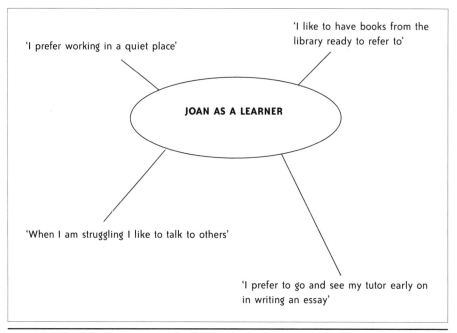

'I like to have books from the library ready to refer to'

'I prefer working in a quiet place'

JOAN AS A LEARNER

'When I am struggling I like to talk to others'

'I prefer to go and see my tutor early on in writing an essay'

3.2 LEARNING PREFERENCES

RESOURCES AND YOUR STUDIES

Joan's story also allows us to look at some important issues about material resources. Such challenges include finding and using books for your studies, word-processing for essays, using computers for research or even having use of a photocopier. These issues may seem small at the moment, but they will prove important in the everyday process of completing your work.

Computers are a resource that you will need to use while studying in higher education. Joan describes how finding a computer to use was a challenge:

> I don't have a computer at home like quite a few of the other people on the course. That meant that I used the ones at school, because it wasn't really convenient to get into the university that often. Because the school is locked up at weekends, I've arranged to stay there some evenings.

To make this arrangement work, Joan had to develop particular ways of working. She started off her work by handwriting it and then typed up work when using computers at her school. To do this she had to be clear about what work she would have to complete when she had access to these resources.

Nicky faced a different challenge to do with using computers:

> When I started the course I wasn't very sure about using the computer. When I wrote my first piece of work I found out it had to be double-spaced, so I went through the whole thing doing each line. I mean, I know how to do it easily now but at the time I didn't know any better.

While Nicky did not have problems with gaining access to a computer, as she went through the course she was learning better how to make use of it. Initially this was challenging for her, but she felt much more comfortable word-processing her work by the end of the course. Even though to start with it was time consuming, she learned the skills through persistence and through sometimes making mistakes.

The challenges Joan and Janet faced in starting to use the library are also two-sided, as the quotes below illustrate.

> *Joan*: I found it a bit difficult with the short-loan books, especially during the holidays because I couldn't get down to return them, and I couldn't take them out for more than a week.

> *Janet*: The library was a bit daunting at first. We had a tour with a guy from the library, but I remember thinking at the end, 'I'm never going to find my way around here'. So what we used to do was go as a group, maybe four of us would go together, then at least between us we could find where we needed to be.

Just as in the example about using computers, Joan and Janet tell us about gaining access to a resource and then learning to use it effectively. At first glance these problems might seem distinct from understanding yourself as a learner, or finding out ways of developing a support network. But they are similar because they show us how, in higher education, you will meet challenges and work through them by learning as you go along. The course you are setting out on is not only about the content of lectures, seminars or books; it is also very much about the skills you will develop on the way. Central to this is learning by doing and coping with practical issues as they arise. All the teaching assistants whose quotes we have used about challenges with resourcing their studies have been successful in overcoming these barriers.

▶ ACTIVITY 3.5

Thinking about some of the resources you need for your studies, do you predict any problems? Jot these down now.

Joan describes an example that shows us how it is important to think about resources before you have any problems.

> We had been using the photocopier on the special educational needs department budget, and then obviously at the end of the year the bill was more than it should have been and the special educational needs coordinator realised it was us who had been using it. In the end it was sorted out, but we just assumed that it would be okay and that people knew we were using it.

In the end Joan's school did help provide a resource to help her and some colleagues in their studies; this was only after the bill had become an issue in the department. In thinking about issues of resources at this early point you might avoid such tension or small problems getting out of hand.

CHAPTER 4

Succeeding and growing in confidence

We have looked at the feelings of apprehension teaching assistants will face in starting out in higher education, and challenges you may have to overcome in choosing to begin a course. Hopefully you also have a sense of the *motivations* that led students to come through these challenges, and the *strategies* they used to overcome them. For many of the teaching assistants we have talked to, this process has been as much about developing their *confidence* as expanding a knowledge or skill base (although these aspects are all linked). This chapter is designed to reflect on those experiences of growing in confidence, and seeks to draw these experiences together and understand how students are becoming more confident.

This chapter, like other chapters in this section, will be based around the experiences of one particular teaching assistant, but it will also draw on the stories of several others as well.

The following are some of the issues that this chapter will raise:

- **Developing confidence**. Examples of how the confidence of teaching assistants has grown through taking part in higher education. This includes:

  (i) *Developing confidence in the workplace*: We examine how teaching assistants feel they have grown in their confidence to develop the work they do in schools.

  (ii) *Developing confidence as a learner in higher education*: This looks at how students have developed assurance in the work they produce.

(iii) *Developing confidence beyond the classroom*: Going to university is a personal challenge, and succeeding is an achievement to be proud of. We will look at how students benefit as individuals from this.

■ **Where does confidence seem to come from?** The previous chapters have addressed the challenges that Janet, Alison and Jill faced, complemented by the voices of other teaching assistants who have been through the experience of beginning study in higher education. This section concludes with a look at the positive experiences gained through a year of studies.

DEVELOPING CONFIDENCE

For those teaching assistants that we spoke to, there were three ways in which they had gained confidence by studying in higher education: first in developing their professional role; second in their ability as a learner in higher education; and third, personally both in and out of work.

DEVELOPING CONFIDENCE IN THE WORKPLACE

Pam describes how she became more involved in the process of learning within her school through taking part in the course:

> I now understand more about what teachers are doing. Before, I was blindly following their lead, whereas now I know the pressures that are on them and I feel that I can make suggestions about how to do things. I feel more confident as a teaching assistant because I see the teaching from the classroom, so I see things as the pupils do, rather than as the teachers do, but at the same time, I am more aware of why teachers do certain things now.

►ACTIVITY 4.1

Pam's comment raises two questions in particular:

■ Pam comments about the difference between teachers and teaching assistants. She feels that part of being more confident is helping her to develop her role as distinct and valuable in the classroom. What aspects of your work in the classroom are distinct from the work of teachers, and are particularly important in helping pupils?

■ From what Pam says, what do you think are some of the ways she has become a better teaching assistant?

It is worth looking at what Pam has to say in some detail. 'I am more aware of why teachers do certain things now' and 'I now understand more about what teachers are doing'. In these statements Pam indicates that she has developed the skills to understand what goes on in the classroom, both in terms of what people are doing, and why they are doing it. Through the course she has become better able to evaluate the actions of teachers and has a firmer grasp of the motivations behind these actions. This is similar in some ways to comments she makes about observing the behaviour of pupils:

> The course really opened my eyes about behaviour, why pupils behave the way they do and what we can do to try and help. I mean, looking behind behaviour. You know, if you can find a reason for it, it's easier to understand how you can help them get over it.

In talking about her work with teachers and pupils, she is now more concerned with looking at the reasoning that lies behind certain actions. She has started to analyse the classroom, and what goes on inside it, in a more reflective and questioning way.

Her comment about working with teachers shows how this helps her to improve her practice in the classroom; she says, 'I feel that I can make suggestions about how to do things'. Pam's confidence has developed in that she is better able to understand the work of teachers and is more willing to try and contribute to the teaching and learning processes. Not only this, but she also feels as though her perspective is different from that of the teacher, and that this makes her point of view a valuable one.

These elements come together in this story showing how Pam's developing confidence greatly helped one pupil:

> I deal with one particularly disruptive pupil. I've tried talking to him, taking him out of lessons. I'd tried all different ways of trying to get through to him, then I spoke to his tutor and to his head of year about him and the school had him assessed by an Ed. Psych. (*sic*) and they found he was dyslexic. But a year ago, I wouldn't have looked at him so deeply; if it hadn't have been for the university course, I would have just accepted him as an awkward pupil and got on with it, but because I'd been on the course, I had the confidence to say something. I didn't know he was dyslexic, but I knew it was worth talking about his behaviour to the head of year. I felt confident to talk to others about him because I now have a better understanding of the pupils, and knew something wasn't right.

Pam's increased confidence and awareness clearly contributed to the assessment of this child. Again we return to the idea that she has developed her insight when she looks at problems. Through looking to the motivations behind this pupil's actions, she has managed to look beyond the surface level of the behaviour itself.

Janet and Maggie also describe their confidence growing in their work with students. However, they emphasise different gains from Pam.

> *Janet*: I'm teaching now; the course has given me the confidence to do that. It's given me confidence in my own ability, I can now stand in front of a class and feel in control.

> *Maggie*: I think I'm more at ease talking to groups and whole class groups as well. The first time I stood up in front the class I just wanted to die. I actually did three lessons over a course of a week and the first one I did I thought 'I'm not going to survive this, and I'm not going to do the second one', but after that I was ready to carry on.

The issues that these two teaching assistants introduce are to do with their confidence when dealing with pupils and, in particular, leading sessions with groups of pupils. They are able to put themselves in a position they would not have felt comfortable with before attending their course.

▶ ACTIVITY 4.2

- The differences between the ideas we have looked at in Pam's case, compared with Janet and Maggie, show that individuals have different areas in which they wish to develop confidence. What areas, related to your work in the classroom, do you think that you would like to develop your confidence in by studying in higher education?
- What areas of your work do you feel really confident in, and proud that you are able to do well?

Gaining confidence isn't just about teaching assistants making changes in the way that they work. In some cases the course helped people confirm that much of what they had been doing was helpful.

> *Nicky*: Sometimes I've thought 'I can't believe that I've been doing totally the wrong thing', and it's given me some alternatives. But on the other hand it has also confirmed that a lot of what I was doing was what I should have been doing anyway but there has been nobody to actually tell you. I've done

it [been a teaching assistant] for seven years but nobody has watched me as far as I am aware, so I could have been doing it wrong for seven years and this has just confirmed that I have been doing some things wrong and shown me ways to get over it, but confirmed a lot of what I was doing was right but just didn't know why.

For Nicky the experience of being observed and assessed was not just seen as a hurdle to get over. The process of going through the course has given her the opportunity to have the good work that she has been doing valued and recognised. It offers her confidence that had not been provided, owing to a lack of other training.

DEVELOPING CONFIDENCE AS A LEARNER IN HIGHER EDUCATION

Having started her studies, Pam was concerned about writing assignments as part of the course. Again it is in her interaction with others that we can see her developing in confidence as a learner as well as a teaching assistant:

The first piece of writing that we had to do I found really difficult, trying to find quotes from books, that sort of thing, doing all the reading and having to pick out the bits that were relevant. I wasn't used to doing that, so I found that difficult to get the hang of. The way I got round these problems was by talking to others and finding out from them how they had done things. What I found was that some of the others had the same problems as me and so we would end up discussing them and that really helped and it meant I didn't feel so isolated.

Having initially been worried about the standard of work that would be expected of her, Pam found the support of people in the same position as her to be helpful, and the attitudes of others to be sympathetic and cooperative. This reiterates a point that we made earlier: you will face challenges similar to those of others on your course.

Alison also felt that her confidence had grown as a learner:

I have gained a lot of confidence. On a personal level I now know I can do it and that has given me confidence, and now I've got the confidence to go on and do the English [teaching] course because I know I can work to what the university wants, so I know I'll be able to do it, whereas this time last year, I would have worried about whether I could have.

Alison feels that her increased confidence will allow her to continue in her future studies as she progresses to train as a teacher.

▶ ACTIVITY 4.3

We address issues of progression in Chapter 12. However, this might be a good point to start thinking about your next steps once you have finished your current course.

- Do you intend to be involved in study in the future? If so, what specific areas do you feel you need to work on in your first experiences of higher education?

This is a difficult question, and in asking it we return to the discussion in Chapter 1 about your motivations to take part in the course on which you are setting out. If your motivations are to achieve a long-term goal (as in the case of the teaching assistants in the last few chapters who wish to go on to become teachers), do you know what the next steps will be? This is important, because study in higher education is generally flexible enough for you to tailor your learning experience to meet your own needs.

For example, should you wish to go on to become a teacher in a secondary school, it may be useful for you to base one of your assignments in the department of the subject you would like to specialise in. Should you wish to develop your skills related to supporting pupils with special educational needs, you may want to set up opportunities to observe individual pupils who have particular needs.

DEVELOPING CONFIDENCE BEYOND THE CLASSROOM

Below Lesley describes that she felt more confident as an individual, and began to see the expectations she should hold of herself differently:

> I used to see other people come onto the staff and be given responsibilities. I'd think 'well, they're the sort that put themselves forwards for things', so I never really thought about it because I felt 'I'm not like that'. Now it's different, I'm not happy with the grotty jobs any more. I mean, I love doing the maths and have made sure that I'm more involved in that. That's what I want to do.

Previously Lesley separated herself from the 'sort of people who put themselves forwards for things'. This separation had meant that while working as a teaching assistant in the same school for three years she had seen people come into the school and move on ahead of her. There is something quite different about the way in which she now talks about her

---

determination to go on and specialise in mathematics. She is much less passive in deciding what choices she will make in her career.

WHERE DOES CONFIDENCE SEEM TO COME FROM?

Each of the stories above gives us an idea of some of the benefits that individuals have experienced while studying. These stories are about working with other professionals in the school setting, being more confident to deal with students in certain ways, developing confidence in learning at an undergraduate level (and feeling able to extend this learning in the future) and developing a personal confidence and assertiveness.

▶ACTIVITY 4.4

To try and gain an overall understanding of this chapter, the following question may be useful to think about.

- If you look at the gains that each of the students has made in this section, where do you feel their confidence comes from?

The quotes from Amanda and Nicky below may offer some help in answering this question.

> *Amanda*: It's very easy as a teaching assistant, before this course, going into a class, doing what you're doing under directions, doing it because it's what you do. Having done this course and having thought about certain aspects of it, you're more inclined to think 'Okay, I know I'm doing this, I know what I've been asked to do, but *why* have I been asked to do it?'

> *Nicky*: I've enjoyed it; it's been really good. I'm not just happy with the 'this is why we do it', I want to know the whys and wherefores.

The teaching assistants are beginning to look at their work and their studies to analyse what their strengths and weaknesses are. The process isn't one of feeling threatened when criticisms are made; rather it's one of recognising areas you need to work on and growing through addressing these issues. Two examples in particular show this. Pam felt unconfident in her ability to write academically; the way she solved this was to be open about the difficulties she experienced, and in doing so she found that others in the group faced similar problems, so they could all provide support for one another. Secondly, Nicky was observed in her work for the first time in seven years. What she gained from this was an element of confidence that much of the work she had been doing with pupils was good, as well as recognising some areas in which her practice could be improved. She shows us that being assessed, and doing work for a higher-education course, are about recognising and valuing your strengths as well as understanding your need to develop.

Their confidence comes from looking at themselves as teaching assistants or learners, *understanding how they can develop*, and then *being successful in making changes* they felt to be positive.

Learning in higher education

Chapter 5: Developing study skills

In this chapter you focus on the basic skills all students need for their studies, including:

- Reading and note-taking

- Learning in the professional context, observing and talking.

- Knowing yourself as a learner

- Linking your course to your work.

Chapter 6: Personal organisation and expectations

To make the transition into higher education you need to address practical issues as well as study skills. These include challenges such as your own personal organisation, and developing an understanding of how your university or college works. The chapter includes:

- Organising and keeping files

- Time management

- Tutorials, seminars and lectures

- Your expectations of your institution

- Expectations held of you

- Resources.

Chapter 7: Meeting assessment criteria

You need specific skills in order to complete assessed work successfully. In this chapter particularly you will learn about writing to criteria. There is also guidance on other methods of assessment, such as making a presentation and developing a portfolio. Topics covered in the chapter include:

- Written assignments such as essays

- Referencing

- Giving presentations

- Developing portfolios for assessment.

CHAPTER 5

Developing study skills

In this chapter you will be asked to think about ways in which you can develop general skills that will be of benefit to you throughout your studies.

While skills such as reading, note-taking and understanding processes of learning will be important to all students, we go on to examine an area that will be of particular importance to teaching assistants. This is: taking ideas explained and suggested on your course and applying them to the classroom. By linking these ideas together (though they may on first glance seem quite separate), we hope to underline a central purpose of teaching assistants taking part in higher education: developing more effective ways of helping students to learn.

The following are some of the issues that this chapter will raise:

- **Developing your reading skills.** This section suggests particular ways you can learn to approach reading that will allow you to better manage your workload.

- **Taking notes.** Recording information so that you can develop your understanding and develop a resource for future reference will be vital. This section will help you to develop techniques for taking notes.

- **What kind of note-taker are you?** You are asked to evaluate what methods for note-taking might be best suited to you.

- **Knowing yourself as a learner.** For students who are on higher-education courses there are particular approaches to learning that can help in being successful. We explore one idea in this section.

- **Linking your course to your work.** You will consider how students we have spoken to and worked with have been successful in developing better practice through their studies.

DEVELOPING YOUR READING SKILLS

Your course will involve gathering and processing a lot of information. In order to do this, it will be crucial to read texts recommended by your course tutors, and to read beyond these essential texts. You may feel overwhelmed by the mass of words, paragraphs and pages you now face, and so it is important to develop skills that will help make the process of reading more manageable. This will help maximise the benefit you gain from what you read.

Let us start by looking at some comments from Pam and Janet, two teaching assistants introduced earlier, to see how they developed their reading skills throughout a year of study at university.

> *Pam*: You have to learn to read quickly ... You have to learn to skim-read because it's impossible to read whole books because you've got to look at so many. You've got to learn to identify the information you need and don't attempt to read every page or even every chapter; pick out the ones that are most relevant.

> *Janet*: I found it difficult at first to read all the material we were meant to, but you've just got to prioritise and read what is really essential, the material that is going to give you the most information.

These quotes draw out two key elements of developing reading skills:

- you have to develop skills in identifying *what* is best to read

- you have to develop skills in *how* you read.

To demonstrate, if you are reading a text from an essential reading list, and identified by a tutor as important, you will need to read it in detail without skipping any sections. On the other hand, if you are reading a book to extend your thinking, you may focus on relevant sections of the book, rather than try to read it all in detail. Similarly, you may select only the relevant sections of a book when developing a point for an essay. However, you may skim-read these in order to focus in on particular points that apply to your essay.

Some authors have suggested techniques for reading and methods for judging how important different texts are. Judging whether a text is important and appropriate will influence whether you decide to read it, and if so, how you read it. Some criteria for judging how helpful you may find particular texts are given in Figure 5.1.

Title	Does it seem relevant?
Author	What is the author's experience? Is the author(s) unknown or seen as an authority?
Date of the publication	Is the book recently published (in the last five years)? If not, are there specific reasons for using an older text? Is it, for instance, a classic?
Publisher (if applicable)	Where is it published? Overseas material might be more relevant on the general international scene.
Contents page (if applicable)	Does it appear to cover issues in which you are interested? Are they relevant to your work?
Information on the back cover and the introduction	Does the information here seem relevant to your purpose?
References	Are these recognisable? Are they comprehensive, indicating that the topic has been well researched? (As your knowledge of a particular area develops, you will become aware of which authors' names you may expect to see.)
Text itself	From a quick scan, is it written in a comprehensible style? (You are much more likely to perform a reading task effectively when you are not put off by extraordinarily formal or jargon-packed text. You may not have a choice in reading material but if you do, find material that you can easily understand and which suits your purposes.)
Bias	Is there any bias? For instance, does a particular company or organisation have an interest in the line of argument presented? If this is the case, consider the value of the text in your argument.

5.1   ASSESSING A TEXT (BASED ON: DE FAZIO, 2002: 69)

In deciding whether a text will be helpful, you may wish to consider some or all of the suggestions in Figure 5.1. The key is to find a system for analysing the writing of other people so that you can (reasonably) decide whether you will read it, and if so, in what amount of detail. However, it is also important to remember that texts on essential course reading lists are there for a purpose, and do need to be read thoroughly.

Once you have decided that a particular text is relevant to your needs, there are some specific techniques you can apply to help you get the most out of the text. Some of these reading techniques are listed in Figure 5.2.

Skim-reading	This involves running through a text quickly to get an idea of what it's about. This should give you a sense of the tone and content of the text, and help you decide whether you need to read it in more detail, or whether a general understanding will be helpful enough.
Scanning	If you are looking for specific information in a text, you may be able to look through it and look for clues as to the sections you will want to read in more detail. For example, using the index to look for sections that mention an author whose work you are keen to know more about, or looking for key words relevant to what you are researching. This may help you find a few paragraphs you are particularly interested in rather than wading through a full chapter.
Reading the first and last sentences of each paragraph	Important information tends to come at the start and end of paragraphs. Information at the start of the paragraph will give you an indication as to what the rest of its contents are likely to be. By reading just the first and last sentence of each paragraph, you might be able to gauge how the argument of a text as a whole is developing or identify important sections.
Reading to improve your writing style	You may look closely at an author's style to see how they structure sentences or paragraphs, how long sentences are, or how they are linked. You may then try out structuring some of your work in a similar way to develop writing that 'flows'.

5.2   TECHNIQUES FOR READING (BASED ON TURNER, 2002: 80–4)

The way you read a text will depend on why you are reading it. Using the reading techniques suggested in Figure 5.2 does not mean that you are cutting corners. It is part of the process of recognising that you have a limited time in which to read, and that to make the most of this time you will not be able to read everything you want to in minute detail.

It is important to remember that some academic writing can be difficult to read for a number of reasons. For instance, you may be unfamiliar with some of the jargon and acronyms the author uses. If this is the case, as you become more familiar with these, you may be surprised at how much easier it becomes for you to read the text. On the other hand, the text may be difficult because it contains new ideas or complex concepts. In this case, topics covered in your course may help you to become familiar with the ideas and understand some of the concepts. As before, these text will become easier over time. When authors are writing in more depth about some of these concepts, you may have to work harder to understand their thinking.

If you are not used to reading professional or academic articles and books, initially you may find yourself struggling to get through even a few pages of a text. If you are reading a more challenging text for your course, try reading around the subject first to get a general idea of the topic, then come back to it when you have done this. You might then find that you have accumulated enough knowledge to make reading the text a helpful and illuminating experience.

Through all these experiences you will find that the process of reading is one that may take some time to get used to. Your reading skills will develop over time, as Pam explains in the following way:

> When we started out I was reading everything too closely, because I hadn't done that sort of thing for a long while and found it difficult. But now I know what I am doing. I spend too long reading sometimes, but I can skim through whole chapters if they don't seem relevant.

Thus, as Pam progressed through the course, she developed a reading level she felt comfortable with. She also developed techniques that helped her to gather information from texts more efficiently.

TAKING NOTES

Reading is an essential element of broadening your understanding of an area. However, as well as reading you also need to develop the ability to condense what you read into a form that will be easy to refer to and that helps you remember the key points. You will need to develop note-taking skills. This includes taking notes from readings as well as recording skills that you can apply when taking notes from seminars or lectures.

Notes act as a means of recording information so that you have a resource to refer to when completing coursework or essays. The process of note-taking can also help you to remember information and understand the topic. Notes should contain the key points you require from a book or lecture in a format that you find easy to record. Your notes should be in a form that allows you to easily understand the information when you read them at a later date. We discuss below two different formats for note-taking and recording information: linear and diagrammatic.

LINEAR NOTES

Linear notes are perhaps the most usual method of note-taking. Because they are sequential, they may be particularly useful when you are taking notes in a seminar or lecture. However, linear notes are not simply continuous prose, they are a series of notes that highlight key points. Linear notes will usually be made under a hierarchy of headings (see Figure 5.3).

MAIN HEADING FOR NOTES

Heading for section of notes 1

Heading for sub-section 1
   Point 1
   Point 2
   Point 3
Heading for sub-section 2
   Point 1
   Point 2
   Point 3
Heading for sub section 3
   Point 1
   Point 2
   Point 3

Heading for section of notes 2

Then continue as above . . .

5.3   SUGGESTED OUTLINE FOR LINEAR NOTE-TAKING

There are several advantages of using linear notes:

- You can make notes in the same order as the book you are reading or the lecture or seminar you are attending. Most academic texts will be in a format consisting of chapters subdivided into sections. Many lectures and seminars will be organised around key points that the lecturer is trying to get across. Because of this it will be fairly easy to make linear notes as you read or listen.

- If your notes are clearly organised you will easily be able to find and refer to specific points at a later date.

■ It is easy with linear notes to include a fair amount of written text and detail, if required. Whether this is helpful will depend on the purposes of the notes you are making. For example, if you are making extended notes for the purpose of essay writing, this could be helpful. If, however, you are trying to create very brief reminders to look over at a later stage, detailed notes will not be necessary.

The main problem with linear notes is that it is difficult to illustrate links between different sections or topics. This is crucial if you are going to work at a higher academic level. Alternative ways of making notes may help you to understand more clearly where different ideas overlap. Techniques such as those included in the following section may prove helpful.

DIAGRAMMATIC NOTES

Diagrammatic notes are often referred to as 'spider' diagrams. The aim here is to give yourself an overview of the area you are studying, on just one side of paper. This can help you gain an overall understanding of a given topic. A possible way of organising such notes is given in Figure 5.4.

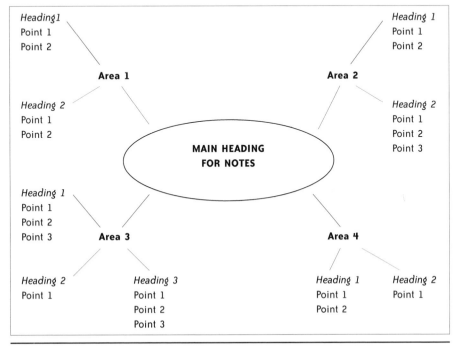

5.4   SUGGESTED OUTLINE FOR DIAGRAMMATIC NOTE-TAKING

There are several advantages of using diagrammatic notes:

- By looking at the page you can begin to get a feel for the topic you are looking at as a whole. You are not looking at isolated 'chunks' of information.

- Quite a lot of information can be included in a diagram, and it allows for information to be linked.

- Because you have organised this information (and therefore made sense of it in your own way), it will help you remember the key points.

- You might find that if you have to draw a diagram about a topic, and think of a way to present the information on a page, you will not just be writing the information down, but you will gain a better understanding of it.

For some people it will be quicker (and more helpful) to take linear notes as they go through their reading. Others will find it quicker to read something in full and then think about making notes in whatever form they find most useful. The important thing about spider diagrams is that they force you into making links and identifying relationships between arguments or ideas.

A particular type of diagrammatic note-taking is the *concept map*, which puts you as the learner in a more active position. In this approach to note-taking, you start with an idea or concept and as you read and develop your understanding, you make notes to record this understanding, rather than summarising the information itself.

WHAT KIND OF NOTE-TAKER ARE YOU?

To start this section, have a go at Activity 5.1.

▶ACTIVITY 5.1

Find a section of a book that you think it is important to understand clearly. Try out the different note-taking ideas we describe above. Different people will find different techniques helpful. Think about:

- Which technique did you find *easiest* when recording the information? Which technique did you find the *quickest* to record the information? Were these two the same?

- While you were writing the notes, which technique helped you to understand the passage most clearly?
- Looking back at the notes, which do you think will be the most helpful if you come back to them in a month's time?

If you find one form of note-taking more helpful than another, this will have an effect on the overall style of how you record information. However, you will find that you take notes in a variety of ways, depending on what you are taking notes about.

KNOWING YOURSELF AS A LEARNER

How can you tell what are good ways of learning for you? What are the best ways of achieving your goals? Several theorists who have tried to understand various ways of effective learning suggest there may be differences between 'surface' learning and 'deep' learning. They have suggested that students who do well in higher education might adopt 'deep' learning processes. Students who only go through 'surface' learning processes tend not to be so successful. But what do these terms mean?

Surface learners tend to look at their studies as 'collecting facts'. However, *deep* learners evaluate and reflect on what they learn, and situate it within their personal understanding. We can see how the latter contributes to more positive learning experiences. An example can be found in the description of types of diagrammatic notes. An exercise that would be likely to encourage surface learning would be to summarise facts in a spider diagram, according to how they are presented by the original author. To engage in deeper learning, you might find it more helpful to develop notes in personalised concept maps.

Turner (2002) suggests further characteristics of deep learners. They:

- make sure they fully understand concepts, ideas, and the relationships between them

- fit what they are working on into an overall framework

- have an enquiring, questioning attitude to what they are reading about/listening to, rather than just accepting facts and absorbing them

- take what they learn and place it into their existing understanding of an area of study, e.g. they don't go into a topic as if their mind were a blank slate.

What does this mean for you as a learner? These ideas suggest that to take part in 'deep' learning you will have to come to your own understandings about topics and concepts (not just accept the understandings of others). You will have to make links between the different areas you are studying in some kind of overall picture (as opposed to learning a list of unconnected facts). This can be quite challenging, especially for people not used to studying. It may mean speaking up in class or following up new and difficult ideas by asking for help.

What is likely to make you take part in deep learning activities? Prosser and Trigwell (1999) describe deep learners as self-motivated, and likely to find learning a reward in itself. They are likely to try and satisfy their own curiosity by, for example, relating ideas to their own experiences and looking for patterns in what they are learning. They recognise broad arguments, but also realise the importance of the elements that make up these larger arguments.

Most people reading this book will be mature students and will have made their own decision to be in higher education. For many, starting a course will be a step towards achieving a personal goal (other teaching assistants describe this kind of motivation in the first chapter of this book). If you can keep these personal aims in mind, rather than seeing the course as an external imposition, your learning is more likely to be rewarding. Also remember that you are studying on a course related to your work. This is really important, because if you are struggling to understand something, place it in the context of 'Where could I apply this to my work?', or 'Where have I seen something like this while at work?'. If you can understand theories you are learning through concrete examples, they are more likely to 'come alive' for you, and they are more likely to be remembered, and you will be able to construct your own understandings.

LINKING YOUR COURSE TO YOUR WORK

The personal steps you will take in learning in higher education should be linked to your professional development as a teaching assistant. This is a process you will have to take part in actively. Ideas you are taught will only be put into practice through experimenting (and sometimes failing) with new ideas in the classroom. You are the person who will have to make the judgement: 'Is this likely to be useful in my work?', and the person who is likely to judge if something new has worked out, i.e. 'Would it be useful to do this again?' Amanda gives us an excellent example of this:

> There was a pupil that I worked with in Year 11 maths, she's left now but then I was actually supporting her in the Year 11 maths. She finds it very hard unless something is in front of her, she finds it really hard to actually visualise what she's doing at all. We had the seminar about learning styles and the research about learning styles made me realise some of her difficulties very much stemmed from not being able to actually see things; tangibly, you can explain to her but unless she can see it she doesn't know how it works. One of the lessons following that was to do with drawing nets that make up a cube once it is flattened. They were drawing nets and the teacher drew a cube on the board and asked the pupils to draw a net of the shape. She had no idea. Although she had the visual in front of her she had absolutely no idea of how this could unfold. Because of realising the connection between learning styles I went to get her a box. I undid the seams of the box and we just laid it out so she could actually see that this is a box; when you put it back up it forms a cube and when you take it apart again it forms the net. It was just something simple to put in front of her but it meant that instantly she could actually see what she was doing, because again it comes into the language thing; you say a net and automatically she was visualising something you go fishing with as well. It's tying the whole thing together; it's the use of language and appropriate visual clues to help her to gain access to a mathematical concept.

Amanda had learned about the theory of learning styles in a seminar, and used this knowledge in the classroom to help a pupil. She had taken the theory, and applied it to an instance in school; the girl struggling with mathematics. This is an example of a way in which you could help yourself to move beyond the surface and develop 'deeper' learning. There are several elements to the way in which Amanda has done this:

- She reached a point in a lesson in which she judged it might be useful to try out putting the theory into action, and tried it out.

- She found a way of translating the theory into a practical idea, opening out the box to explain how to draw a net.

- She linked her knowledge of learning styles to a practical activity in the classroom. In doing so, she used her awareness of the importance of language in using the word 'net', and the images this could raise in the girl's mind.

Through trusting her own judgement that this might be the right time to try something out, Amanda succeeded in helping one of her students by drawing on what she had learned on the course. It could work the other way: you might find that you will try something out and it won't work. This too raises important issues to think about and learn from, because trying out new ways of doing things takes new skills. The first time you have a go, you will not have had any practice. What this means is that if something doesn't work out, you should think about whether this was because it was a bad idea or whether you just need to practise a bit more.

When we talked to teaching assistants who really felt as though they had benefited in their work from what they had learned in gaining a qualification, what they said came down to trying things out with the support of teachers. Are there some suggestions you could make to teachers you work with? By linking your studies and your work in these kinds of ways, you will gather rewards in both.

REFERENCES

De Fazio, T. (2002) *Studying Part-time Without Stress*. Crows Nest, NSW: Allen & Unwin.

Prosser, M. and Trigwell, K. (1999) *Understanding Learning and Teaching: The experience in higher education*. Buckingham: Society for Research into Higher Education, with Open University Press.

Turner, J. (2002) *How to Study: a short introduction*. London: Sage.

CHAPTER 6

Personal organisation and expectations

To make your life easier in higher education there are some practical issues you should be aware of early on. These include organisational tasks such as sorting out your files. They also include points that will help you make the most your teaching, for example, knowing how to prepare for a tutorial.

As your course progresses, you will become more confident about your academic work, and in 'knowing your way around' higher education. If you start out with a few clues about what your experiences are likely to be, and how you can best prepare for them as a learner, the steps to becoming more confident and proficient will be clearer. This chapter aims to provide some of those clues.

The first two sections of this chapter are about organising files and time management. These are largely personal issues. The latter sections of the chapter focus on recognising that although you take part in a course that is provided by an institution (e.g. a university, a college, a School Centred Initial Teacher Training group), you are an active partner in the learning process. As such, if you know some ways for making the most of lectures or tutorials, their benefit can be extended.

The following are some of the issues that this chapter will raise:

- **Organising and keeping files.** This section offers some points that will help you keep and organise files so that they will be a valuable resource to you.

- **Time management**. Thinking about how to manage your time so that you are able to balance studies, work and life outside of these.

- **Tutorials, seminars and lectures**. Preparing for the different teaching styles you will meet in higher education, and how to make the most of each of them.

- **Expectations held of you**. Understanding some of the expectations of you, and expectations you have of the institution you are registered with.

- **Resources**. Gathering together the resources you have to help you with your studies.

ORGANISING AND KEEPING FILES

You need to find some way of organising the notes you take, and other paper you collect on your course. This may sound obvious, but it is important that you find a system that can support your learning. For some people, sets of immaculate files will spontaneously fill their shelves, each of which is carefully labelled and colour coded. For others, reams of note-filled paper will teeter in ever-higher piles on the floor or table, stacked in the order they arrived. Most of us exist somewhere between these two extremes, so the points below should provide some useful reminders. The papers (notes, handouts, documents, articles) you collect should act as a resource for you throughout your studies; it is therefore, important that you are able to find, with relative ease, information you wish to call on. If you can do this, you have a filing system that works.

It is a good idea to plan ahead and buy a set of folders and dividers to put papers in as they arrive. If you manage to do this you won't be constantly 'catching up' to get your files in order. Individual seminars and lectures will normally be part of a broader topic, such as 'Behaviour Management' or 'Inclusion'. If you have a folder for each of these broader topics, you will be able to take the correct folder with you each time and fill it up as you go along. You can then add to these folders; notes from further reading you are asked to do, or any reflections or exercises you are asked to take part in while at work.

The two teaching assistants below highlight the importance of keeping files up to date and organised. They do so with different levels of success:

> *Alison*: I'm really bad at organising myself. I lose things and forget where things are. I would advise anyone doing the course to keep their files up to date. I did keep it all in one place so at least I knew that whatever I'd lost

was somewhere in the pile. It would have been a lot easier if I'd kept everything in some sort of organised way.

Joan: I found I had to organise my work really well. We were given so many handouts and I took so many notes, I found it really important to keep all of these filed and dated and then I could refer to them when I needed them.

The points listed below may be helpful as a starting point in organising and keeping your files. They are not meant to be a list to adhere to rigidly; they are points that you may find helpful. By the time you finish studying you will certainly have ideas of your own that could be added to this list.

- You may want to keep all your lecture notes and personal notes relating to one subject area in one section of a ring binder, using dividers to separate different topics.

- You may find it easier to have a separate ring binder file for each aspect or topic of a course and use different coloured ring binders for each of these.

- Try to make your files easy to understand when you look at them, making good use of colour coding and clear labelling.

- File notes as soon as you are able to, making sure you fill in any gaps in your notes before you file them.

- Date your notes.

- You may find it useful to have a separate section of your file for useful quotes, making sure you include full details of the source of your quote, i.e. author's name, date of publication, title of publication and publisher (see the section on referencing in Chapter 7).

- Keep index cards of what you read. If you also include a reference and very short summary of the text, this can help as a memory aid when you are looking for helpful texts to go back to at a later point.

- You may find it beneficial to devise your own symbols to indicate what your notes relate to; for example, LN = lecture notes, PN = personal notes, BMS = behaviour management strategies. Symbols could be written in the margin, or you could use different coloured ink or highlighters to indicate different sections.

In whatever way you decide to organise and keep notes, the important thing is that you find a system that works for you.

TIME MANAGEMENT

In Section I of this book we introduced teaching assistants who were facing the challenge of balancing their studies with personal pressures and a heavy workload. In order to do this, they were having to make decisions about when they would be able to study, and times when they would make space to be with others or just relax. Figuring out what work you will have to do, how long you will give to it and how you will balance this with other aspects of your life means that 'time management' becomes vital.

The first point is to *be realistic*. Don't try and draw up a plan that will account for your every waking hour, but similarly don't expect to fit your studies in without making some sacrifices in other areas of your life. What might be helpful is to look at the work that you have been set for your course and make an estimate of the time within which you will need to complete it (more than likely there will be some guidelines provided for you). Once you have done this, see if you can save some space in the week that you can dedicate to studying. You will find that if you specify the time you give to your studies, and stick to deadlines to complete your work, time will be spent more productively.

The second point is to *be prepared to be flexible*. Problems do come up, and sometimes a task will take longer than you expect. This shouldn't be a problem provided you leave some space for this to happen. Remember, don't fill up all your time, otherwise you will feel under huge pressure.

The teaching assistants below show that they had to make quite definite decisions about how long they could give to certain tasks. It is important to make decisions like these and stick to them:

> *Alison*: I would like to have spent more time in the library, but I found my time was limited and I had to set myself limitations about how much time I spent on work. So if I knew I only had so many hours to finish a piece of work, then I would just have to get it done in that time . . . I had to be really strict about how much time I spent on things.
>
> *Pam*: The main problem for me was fitting in the studying at home; I just had to find a way of fitting in all the homework you're given. I'd usually work late in the evening . . . I got to the stage when I thought, if things don't

> get done, though! . . . you have to develop a hardness. It's very difficult, but
> I think you have to be determined to do it for yourself and realise that you
> don't have to feel guilty just because you are not running around after
> everyone. You need to set time aside to work: I'd usually go up about
> nine-ish and work then. That's when I felt comfortable about working, we'd
> had our meal, the jobs were done, so I could spend time on work then. I'd
> also get up early at the weekend and work then.

People frequently feel as though they don't have enough time, and this is never more true than when working towards a deadline for an assignment. To help with this, there are some ideas that will help you to manage your time. Firstly, limit the amount of time you spend looking for information. The Internet in particular will provide a seemingly never-ending source of information, and you may experience the same feeling when reading around a topic under study. Give yourself a deadline for reading and researching a topic, after which you will start to write up your assignment. Beware of feeling that you need to keep reading and researching, as this can become a strategy for avoiding writing. You need to recognise this as an avoidance strategy and be strict with yourself. This is a good reason for setting personal deadlines. Secondly, you will need to proofread and edit what you first write for assignments and then re-draft certain aspects. You may well need to give yourself a deadline for completion of your first draft some time before the submission deadline. Not only will this give you some space to edit and rewrite parts, but it may also give you the chance to show what you have written to a tutor or mentor. Thirdly, if you find that you are really struggling with a piece of work, time management can help you. Break down what you have to do into manageable sections or tasks, and set yourself time limits for each section. You may find this helps you to understand the piece of work in a less intimidating way. Also, if you plan when to study, you are likely to feel less stressed about how you are going to get through all of your work.

Once you have decided the amount of time you need in order to complete a piece of work, you can then think of when you will study. The best time to study varies from individual to individual. Some people find it easier to work early in the morning, when the house is quiet, others late at night. Some need silence, while others can work with people and noise around. This means that when planning your study time, it will be important to consider how you work best. For example, it may be better to have regular two-hour work periods with a clear focus and targets, rather than having a whole day during which you may lose concentration and may not achieve so much. It is also sensible to organise breaks in your study time; for instance, plan to complete a set task within one hour and then have a ten-minute break so you come back to your work feeling refreshed. When you settle down to work make sure you have everything you need at hand. For example, if you are working on an assignment, ensure that you have all the literature you need.

Nobody goes through higher education without feeling that they have sometimes got things wrong. You may be under quite a lot of pressure when completing a piece of work for a deadline, and this is the reality of study for most people. However, breaking work down and setting realistic deadlines will help you to complete better-quality work while putting yourself under less stress. This is particularly true of teaching assistants who face busy lives apart from their academic work. With this in mind, it is better to have a realistic strategy for completing your work as this helps to maintain a feeling of control over what you are doing.

TUTORIALS, SEMINARS AND LECTURES

The input you receive from college tutors will come within three or four main types of teaching situation: tutorials, seminars or workshops and lectures. Understanding the difference between these is important and will help you to get the most out of each as you take part in them. A good way to begin to understand each of the terms is to think of them in relation to how active you as a learner will be when you take part.

Lectures involve a mostly one-way flow of information from lecturer to audience, and there will frequently be a higher number of students in lectures than there will be in seminars and tutorials. The chance for students to ask questions will usually come at the end of the lecture, and questions will generally be directed to the lecturer for a response, rather than opened to the group for discussion.

Seminars or *workshops* will usually include some teaching on a pre-designated topic. At the early stages of a course it will probably be from a member of the teaching staff. As you gain experience it is quite likely that students will be required to research and make a contribution to a seminar topic. Seminar groups are normally small and are likely to be opened for discussion following, and often during, the initial presentation. Sometimes a seminar will just be an opportunity for a group to meet and discuss a reading that has been set within the course, or an opportunity to follow up ideas presented in an earlier lecture. The key aspect of seminars is that they are based on discussion, so you will have the chance to talk about and test out your ideas. A workshop usually has a similar structure to a seminar, but with a more practically oriented focus. For example, there may be a chance to try out and explore mathematics games or interviewing techniques, with a discussion focused on ideas, implications and issues arising.

Tutorials will usually be in a one-to-one or small group setting with your tutor. When you are in the roles of 'tutor' and 'tutee' there tends to be a two-way flow of communication. The aim is that the tutor will have the chance to respond to your individual needs or raise any points they feel are important. Interaction in tutorials is greater and more specific than in the other forms of teaching. In this respect you will have a reasonable amount of input to the purpose and content of tutorials.

Figure 6.1 summarises some of the key points that distinguish tutorials, seminars and lectures. By *interactive* we mean the degree to which the 'audience' (you and your colleagues on the course) shape teaching and learning experiences.

Least interactive – audience receive information	

	Lectures:
	    Large audience
	    Set material
	    Students listen, with questions at the end
	    Little chance for interaction with a group

Increasingly interactive	Seminars and workshops:
	    Small audience
	    Some set material, with room for flexibility with questions
	    Students usually able to ask questions throughout
	    Students interact with one another, 'spark' each other off

	Tutorials:
	    Often one-to-one with tutor
	    Students often raise topic of conversation, always responsive
	    Dialogue between tutor and tutee

Most interactive – more conversation-like than lesson-like.	

6.1   LECTURES, SEMINARS AND TUTORIALS

Although it may seem as though the differences above relate to issues that your lecturers have control over, there are important differences for you in the way you prepare for each, and follow up your attendance of each.

In some ways lectures are the mode of teaching in which least is explicitly asked of the student. You will be expected to listen and record what is going on (find out if your lecturer makes available notes relating to what they are saying). Ideally, you should make sure beforehand that you have some understanding of the issues being covered in lectures, or you may struggle to take in what is being said. However, ideas from lectures are designed as a 'resource' to you, and as such the expectation is that you will follow up what you hear with further reading, in an effort to develop your understanding of ideas presented in the lecture. Many lecturers nowadays will email or circulate lecture notes or copies of overheads in advance of lectures. Looking through such notes in advance will be helpful, and they can act as useful resource if you annotate them within lectures. It is also important to do any preparatory reading that is asked of you. If you have been asked to prepare for a lecture by completing some reading beforehand, many lecturers will assume you have done this, and base the pace of their teaching on this. You will struggle if you haven't prepared adequately. You may also struggle if you miss lectures. As Pam explained:

> It's important to be there and try not to miss any lectures. I know it's tempting to think that it won't matter if you miss just one lecture, but they're all important, there are always things you find out at them, things you didn't know and sometimes you are told things you do know, but that reinforces that what you are doing is correct.

In seminars or workshops you will be expected to take part in informed discussion and reflection on the ideas that are being put forward. For most seminars you will be asked to do some reading that will be recommended by your lecturer, or to have considered an issue in your practice. This is important as it means that the seminar group will be able to think about the subject in a meaningful way with some shared understanding of what is being talked about. The important word here is 'informed' – it can be really frustrating if a few members of a seminar group haven't prepared and slow down those of you who have.

Tutorials are there to meet your needs. If you are having any particular problems with your course, or if there is a particular piece of work you would like some support with, tutorials are there for you to seek help. Equally, if a tutor has any issues which they feel are important to talk to you about on a personal basis, this is where they will probably raise them. With this in mind, you may want to provide your tutor with time to prepare for issues you might like to discuss. For example, if you have a piece of work you are worried about, give a draft to your tutor to have a look at well in advance of the time when you will meet. Or, if there is something you have been taught that you find difficult to understand, have some notes ready to talk about (taking two copies can be a good idea). This kind of preparation will mean that you will be able to take full advantage of the most personally tailored teaching you will receive. If in doubt, ask your tutor what you should bring to the tutorial or prepare in advance. The better your understanding of what to expect from tutorials early in your study, the more useful they will be to you.

Bear in mind, whether you are in a lecture, seminar or tutorial, don't be afraid to ask questions. You may be afraid to seem as though you don't know enough, or you may worry that others will think your question is not relevant. The chances are, if you are questioning something, others in the room are also thinking along similar lines.

YOUR EXPECTATIONS OF YOUR INSTITUTION

On starting your course there will be a process of induction, which aims to help you to become part of the higher-education institution. This will include orientation activities as well as more formal procedures such as registration. What you will usually find is that once you have officially registered you will then be entitled to the resources on campus, for example use of the library and computer services. It is important to read documentation sent to you very carefully and find out times when you will be expected to register. If you work full-time you may have to ask about any special arrangements made for working or part-time students.

During induction you should find out about the full range of student support facilities available to you. There are obvious services like the library, but there may also be other services like study support or childcare facilities. You are likely to be given a handbook and it is worth spending time looking through this just to check what resources are available.

Once you are clear about administrative procedures and student support facilities, your main concerns will relate to academic guidance and clear communication in relation to your course. There will be formal descriptions of the course requirements in handbooks. This will include details such as expectations of assessment or attendance. When you start a programme of seminars or lectures it should be clear what the assessment requirements are, as well as what will be asked of you in terms of reading. You should have a sense of the overall direction of the programme.

However, you might still feel that you aren't clear about some areas and then the best thing to do is ask, earlier rather than later. It is likely that your first seminar will be introductory in nature, so make sure that you have read course documentation and ask about anything that is unclear. Your tutor is likely to be the most important person in this.

As time goes by, discussions with tutors about your work should provide feedback about how you are getting on and how to improve your work, particularly in relation to assessment criteria. Inevitably you will feel anxious at times, and at times you may feel as though you aren't quite sure about how you should approach the next stage of your work. It is at these times that it might be good to ask for a tutorial. Alternatively, you might try to speak to the coordinator or convenor of a series of lectures or seminars you are finding difficult. The most important thing is to talk to people if there is something you don't understand.

Finally, if something happens that means a deadline may be missed, or if you feel as though pressures are mounting up, the best step you can take is to seek help early from your personal tutor or from course tutors. The longer any problems are left, the more difficult they are to sort out. There are expectations made of you because you have agreed to the conditions of the course such as deadlines for assessed work. However, if you feel as though you are not coping, support will be available, but you must seek help as soon as possible.

EXPECTATIONS HELD OF YOU

There are perhaps two questions you might like to ask of yourself:

- What are the formal expectations made of me to pass my course?

- What will be the expectations held of me if I am going to make my learning experiences rich and personally rewarding, and which will help me do as well as I can when being assessed?

If you make sure you know the answer to the first question, you are more likely to avoid making any simple mistakes that are the result of you misunderstanding practical and formal arrangements. The second question recognises that you are the most important person in determining how valuable your experience of studying in higher education will be. It is important to attend to both aspects.

For example, in relation to a particular course assessment, the formal requirements or conditions will be set out in a handbook and often reiterated in guidance from lecturers. These will include that you:

- submit the assignment by the deadline set
- meet assessment criteria (this relates to the quality of what you write; criteria for a pass will usually be set out in the course handbook)
- keep to criteria for submission and presentation of the assignments (e.g. that it is double-spaced)
- observe the word length for the assignment
- show evidence of relevant reading.

Beyond these formal requirements, some additional points to help you develop the quality of your work include:

- developing the assignment with well thought-out arguments
- applying extended reading appropriately
- formulating your own ideas based around evidence from the workplace and your reading
- including evidence that you have extended your research beyond the 'core' that is required of you.

By considering your work in this way, beyond the formal expectations that will be held of you, it might be easier to understand how you might move beyond 'surface learning' toward 'deep learning', a distinction made in Chapter 5.

RESOURCES

You have a range of resources available to help you meet expectations and make life easier and more profitable in higher education. It is worthwhile thinking through what some of these are, and the ones that are of most use to you. In Figure 6.2 we lay out what some of those resources might be. You should also be able to extend this list.

▶ACTIVITY 6.1

Look through Figure 6.2. What resources do you have available that could be added to the lists?

Thinking about resources available to you		
Resources outside of university and school	Resources within the university	Resources within school
• Family and friends to encourage and support you • Computer to organise writing • Internet • Public library	• Friends from the university to offer support, share notes/handouts, discuss seminars swap ideas, proofread for you, 'critical friends' • Computers for written work • Somewhere quiet to work • Library • Tutors providing guidance and support	• Colleagues to offer support and advice • Photocopier • Computer
• • •	• • •	• • •

6.2   THINKING ABOUT RESOURCES

There are both personal and practical resources in this diagram. Personal resources include the support offered by family or peers, and practical resources include resources such as having access to a computer. The teaching assistants we met in the earlier chapters of this book also mentioned these important resources when starting a course, and they are certainly issues that you will have to consider. If you are able to make use of the resources available, it will make the expectations that are held of you less intimidating.

Clearly this chapter has not covered everything that you will need to attend to on starting out in higher education. What it hopefully does provide, however, is an overview of some important issues that you will be able to prepare for. The most significant message of the chapter is that if you find ways of organising your work, and making the most of resources and teaching available to you, you will see your preparation pay off in the nature of your learning experiences. The experiences of the teaching assistants we have met so far in this book have given us some examples of this unfolding in their studies.

CHAPTER 7

Meeting assessment criteria

Assessment will take place at various points of your course, and will take different forms. In this chapter we look at three forms of assessment commonly used on courses designed for teaching assistants: written assignments such as essays; presentations; and portfolios.

The reason for including a chapter on assessment criteria in this book is that there are certain ways of approaching these assessment tasks that are likely to help you to be more successful. What we hope to do is give you some ideas that you can try out in practice. In this process of trying out different strategies, and seeing how successful they are, you will begin to develop as a learner. Just as in Chapters 5 and 6, the things that will work for you will depend on what suits you as a learner as well as the kinds of ways you are used to working already. Do hold on to what you know works for you!

This chapter will provide some useful points for getting started. Bear in mind though that the people who will be most able to help you are your course tutors or supervisors, and other students on your course.

In this chapter we will introduce:

- **Written assignments such as essays.** Key points to think about when writing essays from starting to plan, and from beginning to write, through to refining what you have done.

- **Referencing.** Learning how to reference other people's work.

- **Giving presentations.** Ideas to think about in getting ready for and giving a presentation to fellow students or tutors who are assessing you.

■ **Developing portfolios for assessment.** Some points to think about in putting together a 'portfolio of evidence', and some ideas about how to develop your level of work in a portfolio.

WRITTEN ASSIGNMENTS SUCH AS ESSAYS

We deal with the process of writing and presenting essays in detail. This is because the five-step approach outlined could be similarly applied to other assignments. We describe a five-step process of: (i) 'unpacking' titles set for assessed work, i.e. deciding what is being asked; (ii) carrying out research to address the question; (iii) organising a structure for your work; (iv) engaging with the writing process itself; and (v) reading and editing your work.

Essays are a common means of assessment in higher education. The purpose of an essay in relation to your work as a teaching assistant is for you to draw together your experiences as a practitioner, integrate this with appropriate theory, and arrive at a point of view that you are able to justify with the available evidence. We aim to give you some ideas of how you might go about the process of writing. These steps should help you meet the specific criteria of individual assignments (it is important to check these in course handbooks or assignment guidelines you receive).

We suggest a structure that could help you to tackle writing essays. As with many of the other suggestions for studying that have been given in this book, it will become most helpful if you can adapt the structure to suit the way you prefer to work.

STEP 1: UNDERSTANDING WHAT IS BEING ASKED OF YOU

It is best to start by looking at the title you have been asked to write about, and considering carefully what it means. Spending time thinking about this is time well spent, but what does this actually mean? The title is likely to relate to the courses you have been taking and the literature that accompanies them. However, the title will have a particular focus, so you will have to decide what sort of information is relevant, and what is not. Remember, it will not be asking you to repeat everything you have learned on the course; rather, you will be expected to extend and evaluate what you have learned previously.

For example, your title might be: 'Examine ways in which the reading skills of dyslexic pupils might be developed through learning support'.

What does this title mean? What is it asking you to consider? You will find that once you begin to pick out key phrases and words, your focus starts to sharpen. For example we could analyse the question as operating on two levels.

1. The essay is assessing your knowledge of *dyslexia*.

2. To demonstrate this knowledge, the title is asking you to focus on *reading skills* and the role of *learning support*.

It is valid to approach most topics like this. Think of the two questions: 'What areas of my knowledge are being assessed?' and 'How am I being asked to focus my knowledge?'

Once you have begun to break the title or topic down, you might like to think about broad issues that lie behind it. An example in this case would be 'inclusion'. Finally, you might feel it appropriate to challenge some of the ideas in the title. For example, posing questions such as: is it helpful to think of 'parts' of dyslexia (in this case reading skills), or should you think more holistically?

You may find it difficult to do something like this if you feel you know very little about the area of study. However, as we said, the title is likely to relate to an area you have already studied, so you will probably know enough about the subject area to do some initial thinking around the area (going back to your notes at this point could be helpful). In the first instance, you are not trying to write your essay; you are just beginning to unpack the meaning behind the title and address the problems that you will ultimately have to be able to answer. You might find it helpful to record your thoughts in a spider diagram or concept map (see Chapter 5), which can provide a structure with which to develop your writing.

STEP 2: FINDING THE INFORMATION YOU NEED TO ANSWER THE QUESTION

You will need to begin to research some of the broad areas you identified in Step 1 in more detail. The first places you should look are your notes from seminars and lectures as well as the key readings that were given to you for these. This is a filtering process as you decide which notes and readings directly address the essay title, and which can be disregarded.

Once you have done this, you may wish to extend your reading in certain areas. For example, you may go to the Internet for further information or go to the library for any additional books or articles that might be helpful. When you look at the references made in literature you read, you will find links to other texts that broaden your knowledge base. Being clear about the question and keeping it in mind will help you to focus your reading to those sources that will be directly relevant.

It can be helpful to sort sources of information (e.g. books, articles, documents, etc) into three piles:

1. Really useful, interesting and relevant to the way in which you will address the title. These are sources that you will definitely include in your essay.

2. Interesting, with bits and pieces that are useful and relevant. You will include references to some of these sources in your essay (remembering to hold a tight focus to your title).

3. Interesting but not relevant. Once this pile is constructed, do your best to ignore it. It may have lots of interesting material you would like to read but are they relevant to the title? No! That is why they are in this pile.

During this stage of writing your essay, you will have to put some of your note-taking skills into action as the challenge you face is to draw together different sources that will be relevant in addressing the title. You may end up with information from several sources, but you will need to bring it together by linking the information in a way that does not involve repetition.

▌ STEP 3: ORGANISING WHAT YOU KNOW INTO A STRUCTURE

Facing blank paper is very challenging for all writers. The first thing to do is take control of the situation. Look at the required number of words and work out approximately how many pages this entails (there are about 250 words on a 12-point double-spaced page). Allow one-third of the word length for your introduction and conclusion together, and leave the remainder for the main body of your essay. Figure 7.1 suggests a three-part structure for an essay.

Introduction	The main body of your essay	Discussion and conclusion
'Set the scene', clearly stating what the essay is about and providing an overview of how you will try and answer the question, perhaps defining key terms.	What goes here depends on the nature of the question. Roughly speaking, this section will include the evidence from which you will be able to draw conclusions (this could include references to literature as well as your own experiences). You are trying to give a sense that you have researched the area you are writing about, and that you understand the key related issues. As such you will be expected to present a balanced account demonstrating that you have thought through a range of points of view and related the key issues to professional contexts as appropriate.	This is the point to summarise the different sides of the argument and outline why you have taken a particular stance. It could also be the place where you critically evaluate the question you are being asked to explore. Finally it might be helpful to reflect on your learning process in the time you have written the essay.

7.1   THINKING OF AN ESSAY IN THREE PARTS MAY BE HELPFUL

You should not be too mechanistic when writing assignments for higher education. If it looks as though you have applied a set formula to what you have written, your piece of work will suffer. However, it might be useful to stick to a three-step structure for tackling the task so you are in a position to plan out what you will write. This may be especially helpful for your first few essays.

You should now be in a position to begin planning your assignment in more detail. You will probably find it helpful to break the essay down with sub-headings and it can be a useful process to map these out before you start writing. This will make you analyse what you are going to write in an organised way before you start writing, and will make it easier to develop a picture of what your essay will look like. It will also make your finished piece more coherent.

STEP 4: WRITING

Starting to write your essay in full may involve a few false starts, so allow time for this process. Even the most experienced writers, when faced with that empty page, suddenly discover the need to make yet more phone calls or make another cup of coffee. You should have all the information you need to refer to on hand, along with pens, pencils, paper, etc., and an outline of the structure you will write to. Sometimes it can be an idea just to start writing, not worrying too much about the wording or about how good it is at this stage, but just getting down some ideas. With luck, you will eventually find yourself carried along with what you are writing. You can then go back and edit the start of the essay.

The main thing to remember is that an essay is not the place to simply state your opinions. Yes, your argument should become apparent in the essay, but you must be able to substantiate what you say. Sometimes it will be enough to refer to your experiences, but this will not carry you through an entire essay. You must show that you have reached an opinion through the evidence you understand, and part of this is considering the pros and cons of alternative positions. If you find yourself writing things like 'I think' or 'in my opinion', be careful. Stop and evaluate whether you can back up your position with evidence. If you can, then you will begin to develop a more academic writing style.

If you feel unsure about the way you are writing, you might like to show some of the work you have done to a tutor. They will be able to give you some initial thoughts about writing style and content. It is better to get someone else's thoughts at this early stage before you have written your essay in full. This was an important step for Janet:

> I think we all struggled a bit with writing work that was going to be assessed, but don't be afraid to ask for help. It's not easy getting to grips with an academic style of writing.

STEP 5: READING AND EDITING

This is a very important part of the writing process and is one good reason to manage your time carefully. You will need to allow time to draft and re-draft your work. Pam described her way of working:

> When you're writing, you've got to draft, you can't just write up. I found it useful to use a computer . . . What I used to do was type a draft and then print it out. I found it difficult to work on the computer; I liked to be able to read the work when it was printed out, then I'd go through and edit it by hand, then make the changes on the computer, then I'd print and edit again. I'd maybe do this four or five times until I felt happy with it.

If you have been writing quite intensively, you will find it hard to read what you have written carefully, and to get an overall sense of the essay. Once you feel as though you have finished your essay, try to allow time to stop and give yourself some space from it. Then, after a break from it, read through your work from start to finish. Don't do too much editing at this stage; you are trying to get a feel for whether the essay 'hangs together'. This means understanding whether the essay jumps around between different points or whether you deal with arguments in a coherent way and link them together, rather than merely listing a string of facts. Think also about whether you have 'evaluated' the claims of different authors or just accepted what they have to say on face value. There may be times when you haven't agreed with the author; this is fine providing you can justify your viewpoint.

It is usual to be told the maximum number of words your essay should be, and it is important to stick to the word length as closely as possible. It is important to check guidelines you have been given, as some institutions will give you 10 per cent leeway, while others will ignore any content over that length. At first you may well think you will never write enough, but as you start the writing process it is easy to write too much. In such cases, you will need to edit your work by omitting any unnecessary words or phrases and omit any repetition. This process often improves the work considerably, making, as Joan found, what you say more succinct:

> I found it hard to keep to the word length . . . It's really important to read
> and re-read your work to cut out the words that are not important.

The next stage is to go through carefully looking for any spelling mistakes or poorly worded sentences. As you read through, if there are any points where you find yourself having to go back and read through a section several times, then it is likely that someone else will have problems too. A good tip is to read your work out loud. Any parts that are unclear will become very noticeable. This stage is a process of 'fine tuning'.

If you are the only person who has read your work so far, this is another excellent point at which to ask a tutor or a 'critical friend' to look through what you have done. You will find that another pair of eyes will have quite a different perspective. You may decide to be a 'critical friend' for another course member. Remember that they may present their work in a different way to you, but both may be equally acceptable. As Joan put it:

> I think everyone writes differently . . . It's important to remember that if you
> present something in a different way to someone else, it is not necessarily
> wrong, just different.

Once you feel you have produced the finished essay, have a break. Read through what you have written carefully and see that you feel comfortable handing in the essay. Make any final adjustments and produce your final draft to submit in a form which conforms to guidelines you have been given (complete with title page, references, and appendices if you have them). Check through one final time, making sure all the pages are there, and that the presentation is good. This includes checking that you have been consistent with the presentation; for example, if you choose to write your titles in bold print, all titles should be written in this way.

REFERENCING

When writing essays or doing other work in higher education, it is fine to use the work of other authors to help you explain points you wish to make. Indeed, this is usually expected in assignments. You can do this by either simply referring to the work of another person or by directly quoting from somebody else's work. If you do use the work of other authors, there are two things to remember. First, you can only gain so much credit for having found out the views of others – what you need to do is take a range of views and evaluate them in a way that shows you have come to an understanding of the topic. Second, you must acknowledge the work you use by referencing it.

The point of referencing is so that readers know which authors' work you have read to inform your ideas, and so that they can trace the work should they wish to use it themselves. When referencing you will need to know the title of the chapter (for edited collections), book or article, the author(s) name(s) and initials, the year the work was published, the publisher and the page number relating to any direct quotes. It is a good idea to keep a record of this information for any work you want to reference when you are making notes for your essay, so that you can avoid having to search through books and articles you have already read, just to find out reference details. Here's what Joan said about referencing:

> You need to be really organised with your referencing and keep note of everything; some people got into a real mess and ended up having to go to the library specially to check their references. I kept a book of references and quotes I thought may be useful, so I used to refer to that if I needed to.

The Harvard system of referencing is commonly used in educational texts.

Using this system the citation is written within the text, not in footnotes. This means that you include the last name of the author and the date of publication within the text. Then, at the end of your piece of work, you should give full references, in alphabetical order, of all the work you have used in your writing. This book uses the Harvard system.

If you paraphrase or refer directly to what an author says or argues in your text (but you don't directly quote them) put the author's last name and date of publication in brackets. For instance:

> Learning situations should connect what happens in school to wider opportunities for education (Bentley, 1998).

When you are not actually quoting an author but you are using their ideas, put the last name of the author in the text and the date of publication in brackets:

> Epstein (1995) gives six types of involvement that examine the ways in which parents and schools may work together . . .

If there are two authors, include both of their names (you should also use initials if more than one author of the same name is cited in your work). If there are more than two authors, use all their names the first time and thereafter use 'et al.'. For example: Mannion *et al.* (2000).

If directly quoting from a text, you must include the author, the year of the publication and the page number. For example:

> There is a 'soft rhetoric of partnership' (Vincent and Tomlinson, 1997: 362) that dominates at school level.

If the quotation is more than a very short sentence, or section of a sentence, you should set it out like a new paragraph. The quotation should also be indented and could be italicised.

You should include full references at the end of your text. Below we can see the format in which you will be expected to give these references.

When referencing a book:

Author's last name(s) and initials. (Date of publication in brackets) *Title of book in italics*. Location of publishers: publisher's name.

For example:

Hallgarten, J. (2000) *Parents Exist, OK!? Issues and visions for parent-school relationships*. Southampton: IPPR.

When referencing an edited collection, you need to refer directly to the chapter the author wrote. Remember, the authors write the individual chapters and the editor draws together the collection. You should use the following format:

Chapter author's last name(s) and initials of chapter authors. (Date of publication in brackets) 'Title of chapter in single quotation marks'. Last name(s) and initials of editors (ed.) *Title of book in italics*. Location of publishers: publisher's name.

For example:

MacBeath, J. and Gray, D. (2001) 'Lochgelly North Special School'. Maden, M. (ed.) *Success Against the Odds – Five Years On: Revisiting effective schools in disadvantaged areas.* London: Routledge Falmer.

When referencing a journal article, the approach is similar:

Authors and initials. (Date of publication in brackets) 'Title of article in single quotation marks', *Name of journal in italics,* journal volume number (journal part number): page numbers of article.

For example:

Vincent, C. and Tomlinson, S. (1997) 'Home school relationships: the swarming of disciplinary mechanisms?' *British Educational Research Journal,* 23 (3): 361–377.

All of these types of reference should be included in your reference list, arranged in alphabetical order. If you are ever unsure of how to format a reference, have a look at the reference list at the end of a book, or a reading list given to you for your course.

GIVING PRESENTATIONS

You may be asked to give a presentation to the rest of your group. This may be to share ideas, or it may also be an assessed part of your coursework. Presentations normally take the format of an 'input' to an audience, followed by a more interactive space for questions and discussion. Pam and Janet approached giving presentations quite differently, but both felt similar rewards having given a successful presentation:

> *Pam:* I found them [presentations] nerve-racking. But, after you'd done it, you felt really good; it's like you'd done something you'd never have attempted if you hadn't been on the course.

> *Janet:* I found this OK because I'd grown in confidence . . . On the course we did a presentation as a group; we all pooled our resources and just got on with it. Before I started the course, I would never have anticipated that I could actually do something like that.

The key to giving a good presentation will be how well you prepare, and there are some points you might like to consider.

- First, you will have to carry out research for your presentation and break the topic down into sections. Each section should include one area of your topic. The sections should be focused, contain relevant facts, and where appropriate, alternative views and illustrations (the initial steps for tackling essays described earlier in this chapter might be useful here).

- Decide how you are going to present your material. For example, do you want to prepare visual aids, overhead transparencies (OHTs) or a computer presentation? Bear in mind, though, if you use any of these ideas your aim is to explain ideas in a manner that is as simple to understand as possible. Being over-elaborate in how you try to say something can detract from what it is you have to say.

- When you start your presentation, it is a good idea to lay out your aim or purpose and some of the key areas it will cover. This gives your audience some idea of what they can expect and the structure of your presentation.

- You may use bullet points to show what you are going to talk about and then expand on these brief points as you speak. This can be really helpful as it gives you and the audience an order of key points that you can come back to if you feel you are losing your way.

- Make sure any pictures, diagrams, writing or objects you intend to use in your presentation will be clearly seen by all your audience.

- Don't try to show too much written information prepared for your audience. They should be able to quickly scan any page you show them and pick up an outline of what you are saying. It is up to you to fill in the picture with what you say. Too much information on a slide is much worse than too little.

- Finally, make sure your presentation fits into the time allocation you are given. If you are unsure, do a run-

through without an audience, taking time to display any
visuals and speak as though you are presenting. If you are
giving a presentation in a group, a rehearsal is a good idea:
as well as getting your timing right you will look more
professional if you know who is responsible for which
parts of a presentation.

When you come to give a presentation, you can draw on your teaching
experience. Bear in mind the common-sense points from these experiences: project your voice, and speak to the whole room. Don't read directly
from notes or OHTs for long periods of time, but instead use them to
highlight the main points of your presentation, or as a mental jog for
yourself.

You should structure your presentation so that you introduce the areas
you will speak about, give the bulk of what you have to say, and then sum
up and conclude. The conclusion is important as it should draw together
the key themes and make clear the overall argument or point of what you
have said. It will be your final word, so make sure it is well put.

DEVELOPING PORTFOLIOS FOR ASSESSMENT

You are likely to be assessed for at least part, if not all, of your course of
study by portfolio. As teaching assistants on higher-education courses are
often studying and working at the same time, compiling a portfolio can
be an effective way of gathering experiences from school and reflecting on
these with what has been learned on a course.

A portfolio presents a story of your progress and achievements, as a result
of your being reflective, self-evaluative and critical about your learning.
When you are constructing a portfolio, you 'own' your learning experience because the idea is that the relationship between your curriculum,
assessment and the way that you learn is made explicit. In other words,
you make decisions about what to include in your evidence.

Val Klenowski (2002) sets out six principles to underpin the use of
portfolios. She suggests that portfolio assessment: promotes a new
perspective on learning; is a developmental process; incorporates analyses
of achievements and learning; requires self-evaluation; encourages student
choice and reflection on work; and engages teachers or mentors as
facilitators of learning.

The following points expand on some of these ideas and will be helpful in developing your own portfolio.

- *Portfolio writing is a developmental process.* This means that as your understanding and skills develop, so should your portfolio. You will usually be expected to put a portfolio together over an extended period of time (a university term, for example), so you will have the chance to go back to ideas or work you have included and extend them. Your portfolio should reflect the fact that you are learning, so once you have included something, don't think of it as fixed. Keep questions in your mind like: do I now have examples of work I have done that is more advanced or better illustrates what I am trying to show? Do I more clearly understand a theory I was trying to explain in my portfolio? Don't be afraid to replace! In this way portfolios give you a chance to really think about the learning you are going through and a chance to demonstrate that learning very clearly.

- *Portfolio writing encourages student choice and reflection on work.* Clearly you will have a huge number of experiences from your work in classrooms to draw on in developing a portfolio. You may have to draw on these to show you are performing certain kinds of task and to give examples of the application of ideas or theories suggested on your course. Your choice of what to include in your portfolio depends on the criteria you are being asked to meet but you will have to decide which best show your learning or level of work. However, you will not only have to describe what you have done. Your work should also be analytical. An example may be helpful to explain this.

In the portfolio that Alison was compiling, one element was to 'Produce a record of four pupils working in different ways. Choose one pupil, and show how the learning style the pupil is being asked to use is a) active, b) appropriate for that child's learning and behaviour.' Alison's record of the four pupils was built up over one term and she was able to go back and reflect on her observations in the light of her course. As the term went on, she developed her understanding of 'active learning' in seminars and reading, and added in quotes to demonstrate that what she observed could be given this title (see Figure 7.2).

In a recent history lesson the learning activity was to design and make a castle. This activity was appropriate for Jamie as it was a physical and tactile task. This made the learning style more appropriate for Jamie's learning behaviour, as he was given a higher degree of control over the learning process. This is in agreement with the comment that:

'The teacher's role is one of setting up learning experiences in which pupils are active and have a marked degree of control over the work they undertake.' (Kryiacou, 1996)

By giving Jamie the opportunity to build a castle, he could visualise and be in control of his learning experience. The activity was made active by using computers and creative materials, for example cardboard and paint, which allowed him to participate and as a consequence, take part verbally during the class discussion afterwards. Turner highlights the importance of using materials and tools within classes. This agrees with a definition of 'active learning'.

'In a simple sense it is learning by doing as opposed to being told.' (Turner, 2001)

7.2 EXTRACT FROM ALISON'S PORTFOLIO

- *Analyses of achievements and learning.* To achieve this you have to develop the ability to think of yourself as a learner. Although in Figure 7.2 Alison does describe and evaluate the observations of Jamie that she made in the classroom, she does not describe the learning process *she* took part in to come to these understandings. Although we are looking at the quote out of context from her portfolio as a whole, the *process* of reaching this understanding is not made explicit. Describing the processes of learning you have been through allows your readers access to your developing understanding and can help you recognise the achievements you have made. In this extract, Alison could have started to do this if she had, for example, reflected on how she had come to notice Jamie's learning experience in the first place. (There is an example of how this could be done on pages 114 and 115.)

- *Portfolio writing engages teachers or mentors as facilitators of learning.* It may seem that this point about teachers or mentors does not relate to you. However, what this means is that your tutor works with you to develop the quality of work in your portfolio. It is a good idea to discuss your portfolio with your tutors so that, as with any assessment task, the process of talking with others and allowing others to make suggestions will enable you to produce a better piece of work.

- *Self-evaluation.* The previous points discussed all overlap in some ways, and in many ways self-evaluation underlies them all. Self-evaluation means understanding your current position as a learner, understanding attainable goals to work towards, and steps you will have to take to move between these two.

▶ ACTIVITY 7.1

Use some of the points in Figure 7.3 to help you think about building your portfolio.

Use all the time you are given to put your portfolio together rather than leaving it to the last minute.	All of the points in this chapter about developing the level of your portfolio writing depend on you having the chance to develop your work over time. If you hurry together your evidence, you will not have the opportunity to reflect on, or share your work. Also remember that if the tasks you have been set for your portfolio are designed to be completed over a long period, you will leave yourself with a huge task by waiting until the last minute!
Look carefully at the criteria by which you are being assessed and what you are being asked to show or develop through the portfolio.	You will have guidelines about the areas in which you are being assessed. It is crucially important that the evidence you provide and the theories you use directly relate to those criteria. Check through the areas in which you are being assessed, and the specific criteria. Make sure you understand them clearly before you start compiling your portfolio. If you are unclear in any way, make sure you talk to your tutor and clarify what is being asked for. Ask yourself why you have selected an entry. What does it illustrate?
Make sure you select carefully what you include in your portfolio and focus your content clearly.	It is very easy to produce a huge portfolio. As you gather material over a period of time, the volume of material will rapidly expand. Look back over what you have compiled and check that what you have included is directly relevant, that you are not covering the same point several times, and that you have been analytical in your work.
Think carefully how to present your portfolio.	You may have a fixed format in which to present your work. However, if this isn't the case, make sure that anyone who reads your work can identify where you are meeting assessment criteria. This helps you demonstrate to the reader that you are meeting assessment criteria, and it will also help you check through what you have done and what you still need to do.

7.3   BUILDING YOUR PORTFOLIO

Portfolios are often an opportunity to demonstrate how your work in school has developed, as part of the work you are doing for your qualification. As well as demonstrating your learning to others, this can provide you with a space in which to reflect on your own learning and identify areas in which you feel as though you could develop further. If you engage with a portfolio in this way, you will find that not only does the quality of your assessed work improve, but you will also better understand your own professional development.

REFERENCES

Bentley, T. (1998) *Learning beyond the Classroom: Education for a changing world.* London: Routledge.

Epstein, J.L. (1995) 'School/family/community partnerships: Caring for the children we share', *Phi Delta Kappan,* 76 (9): 701–11.

Hallgarten, J. (2000*) Parents Exist, OK!? Issues and visions for parent-school relationships.* Southampton: IPPR.

Klenowski, V. (2002) *Developing Portfolios for Learning and Assessment: Processes and Principles.* London: Routledge Falmer.

MacBeath, J. and Gray, D. (2001) 'Lochgelly North Special School'. In Maden, M. (ed.) *Success Against the Odds – Five Years On: Revisiting effective schools in disadvantaged areas.* London: Routledge Falmer.

Mannion, G., Allan, J. and Nixon, J. (2000) *Finding Local Prospects in a National Prospectus: Frameworks for thinking about educational purposes. Evaluating new community schools.* University of Sterling.

Vincent, C. and Tomlinson, S. (1997) 'Home school Relationships: the swarming of disciplinary mechanisms?', *British Educational Research Journal,* 23 (3): 361–77.

Developing professional skills and knowledge

This section moves on from the previous two. It takes three aspects of education with which you are likely to be familiar in your work in school, and aims to encourage you to think more widely and critically about them.

Chapter 8: Implementing national strategies

In this chapter there is an introduction to the school curriculum, and how and why curriculum development is achieved in schools, using as examples the National Literacy and Numeracy Strategies and Key Stage 3 Strategy.

Chapter 9: Inclusion: do we know what we mean?

In this chapter you will draw on your own school experiences in thinking about inclusion, and what it means for you and for others in school. You will also explore generic issues relating to inclusive schooling and be encouraged to consider some of the challenges of inclusion, through critical reflection on your own practices.

Chapter 10: Thinking about behaviour management

Everyone who works in schools thinks about behaviour management at some time or other. Some people think about it a great deal, especially when they work with pupils who may present them with more challenging behaviour. This chapter introduces you to some approaches and ways of working with pupils that may help you in your work as a teaching assistant.

CHAPTER 8

Implementing national strategies

One thing that seems certain is that change is a constant feature of life in schools. In this chapter you will begin to understand how and why this happens. We will explain the background to the National Curriculum in England and Wales, the Literacy and Numeracy Strategies at Key Stage 2, and the Key Stage 3 Strategy. We will also discuss some of the implications of the curriculum being organised centrally by government.

This chapter covers the following topics:

- **Why do we have a National Curriculum, and what does it include?**
- **Curriculum development in schools**.

WHY DO WE HAVE A NATIONAL CURRICULUM, AND WHAT DOES IT INCLUDE?

Many countries provide schools with a specification of what pupils should learn. England and Wales have been fairly late compared with other countries in establishing a National Curriculum, as it was introduced for the first time in 1988. Until then, the only subjects required by law to be taught in schools were religious education and physical education. Nothing else was compulsory, not even mathematics or English. Of course most schools did teach these subjects, along with other subjects such as science, music, art, history, geography and European languages; however, these were not compulsory and so there was quite a lot of variation between schools.

▶ ACTIVITY 8.1

Think back to when you were at school. Which subjects can you remember being taught? How similar are these to the subjects you support today?

Depending on your age, you may not have learned information and communications technology (ICT) or design technology. Almost certainly you would not have studied citizenship as a subject. You might remember civics, needlework or home economics, typing or childcare if you are a woman; technical drawing, woodwork or metalwork if you are a man. If you went to a selective grammar school you may have studied Latin as well as French or German.

By the mid-1980s, the UK was falling behind its economic industrial competitors as well as having an increasing problem of unemployment, particularly among young people. The government at the time decided that one problem was the lack of a sufficiently skilled workforce, particularly in new technologies, mathematics, science and communications. Education came into focus as the means by which the skills and aptitudes needed by the country could be strategically developed. This was new thinking, as until then it had been schools themselves who were free to provide curricula as they saw most fitted the needs and aspirations of their own students. Now, the government was suggesting that in the national interest there should be a nationwide collective approach to education.

Up until this time, the schooling received by many people was a matter of serendipity or luck, in many cases inappropriate for individual needs, and sex-stereotyped or narrow. For example, girls, particularly those not selected for grammar schools or top streams in comprehensive schools, tended to study non-academic subjects such as childcare or home economics. Bright working-class girls often dropped more academic subjects in order to pursue clusters of 'vocational' options. These girls were often wasting their time, as they were repeating at school skills that were learned at home. Meanwhile their male counterparts studied woodwork, metalwork or technical drawing at a time of diminishing opportunity in relevant industries. Pupils identified as highly achieving academically tended to study academic subjects without much awareness of how these subject choices would affect options for further and higher education and eventual career choice; an economic recession meant that jobs were no longer secure. A National Curriculum sought to establish a principle of equal opportunity so that each child, no matter where they lived or the background they came from, should have the same access to the same subjects. Within the National Curriculum, subjects were carefully chosen to reflect the needs of the society nearing the end of the century, by providing breadth of knowledge, skill and understanding, and by discouraging early specialisation. It was hoped that this would produce more young people with flexible skills for turning towards the different employment situations they were likely to face.

During the early 1980s, teachers took action about low pay and poor conditions of service in schools by ceasing unpaid voluntary activities, such as lunch duty. This action (one-day strikes resulted in children being sent home) coincided with other industrial action (for example, the miners' strike of 1984) and racial tension in the inner cities. The Conservative government was determined to limit the power of teachers, and establishing control through a new curriculum was a means of doing so.

Worried by the apparently poor examination results of children in comparison with those of countries such as Germany, the government was also determined to monitor the achievement of children regularly throughout their schooling. The problem was that in order for this monitoring to be accomplished, all the pupils needed to have similar school experiences, i.e. there had to be a common curriculum taught in order to test it. This killed two birds with one stone, as comparisons between pupils would inevitably lead to comparisons between teachers and between schools, and such competition would discourage teachers from industrial action (Chitty and Dunford, 1999).

Examinations had been established originally for the most able pupils. They were then used as a means of discriminating competitively between these pupils for such things as career opportunities or entrance to university or college. Proliferation of exams had begun during the 1960s with the introduction of the Certificate of Secondary Education (CSE), an examination to cater for those not aiming for O-level. The CSE and O-level examinations were superseded in 1986 by the ubiquitous General Certificate of Secondary Education (GCSE). The GCSE was originally intended to be one examination, so as not to differentiate between pupils too soon, and was intended for the top 60 per cent of the population in the school year of their sixteenth birthday. This left a long tail of 40 per cent 'unexaminable' children. The government resolved to shorten the tail by a programme of testing throughout the school years. Hence, the National Curriculum was introduced to provide a national diet that could be assessed regularly by state examinations. The testing system remains the most contentious aspect of the National Curriculum to this day.

▶ ACTIVITY 8.2

Think about some of the pupils you support. Which of them benefit from regular testing? Which of them do not benefit?

The National Curriculum in both England and Wales sets out the content and standards of the curriculum for pupils in compulsory education in state schools (Different arrangements apply in Scotland and Northern Ireland). It is divided into four key stages covering compulsory schooling. For subjects within each key stage it sets out programmes of study. There are some differences between the curricula for England and for Wales, and you should check subjects taught in your country. Each key stage covers a particular age range. Religious education is not a National Curriculum subject, but schools must teach it to all pupils. Each subject is set out as a hierarchy of knowledge, skills and aptitudes that school pupils should have acquired by specific ages. Unlike some other countries, children in England and Wales automatically progress through school beginning at age four in Reception, age five in Year One, continuously until they reach Year Eleven in the school year of their sixteenth birthday. Occasionally, children may be accelerated one year if they show particular aptitude in the core subjects, but rarely are they held back a year if they fail to make the required progress. Testing takes place at seven, eleven, fourteen and sixteen against attainment targets that are set, specifying what pupils are expected to know. Thus each of the four key stages is age-related, with a spread of attainment expected in each. Figure 8.1 shows how this works.

Range of levels within which the great majority of pupils are expected to work		Expected attainment for the majority of pupils at the end of the key stage	
Key Stage 1	1–3	at age 7	2
Key Stage 2	2–5	at age 11	4
Key Stage 2	3–7	at age 14	5/6[1]
[1]Including modern foreign languages.			

8.1 RANGE OF LEVELS WITHIN WHICH THE GREAT MAJORITY OF PUPILS ARE EXPECTED TO WORK, AND EXPECTED ATTAINMENT

▶ ACTIVITY 8.3

Open the National Curriculum websites (http://www.nc.net/home.html for England, and http://www.accac.org.uk/publications/ncorders.html for Wales) and find one of the subjects you support. Spend a few minutes familiarising yourself with the curriculum for this subject. How is it set out? What are the legal requirements that teachers must adhere to? What are teachers able to make decisions about themselves?

You will notice that the curriculum is written so as to provide descriptions of the levels of attainment for each subject. Thus, testing at the end of each key stage is designed to check whether pupils have acquired the knowledge, skill and understanding for a particular level. These tests, officially called National Curriculum tests, are known generally as 'SATs'. Theoretically, as everyone should be able to make progress from his or her previous level, it is possible for everyone eventually to reach the next level, given enough time. This form of assessment is called 'criterion referenced', as any single individual is measured against the criteria for a particular level – rather like the driving test, which anyone can pass provided they can perform all the manoeuvres. Once a pupil has achieved a level, this means theoretically (although this is never straightforward) that the pupil and the teacher know what the pupil actually can do. Criterion referencing differs from the system called 'norm referencing' in which, broadly speaking, examination candidates are marked against each other; for example, those achieving the highest marks achieve grade A, regardless of what their marks actually are, and the candidates with the lowest marks are awarded the lowest grades.

The two approaches, criterion referencing and norm referencing, are quite different and lead to a great deal of confusion, especially at GCSE examination results time. Politicians and many parents never seem clear as to why more pupils achieve higher grades – does this mean the standards of pupils' work have gone up because more have met the criteria, or down because the examination standards must have been lower for more pupils to be successful?

CURRICULUM DEVELOPMENT IN SCHOOLS

A curriculum that is designed to meet the needs of a changing society cannot stay the same for long. In the case of the national curricula for

---

England and for Wales, changes to this have come about because of a variety of factors. These factors are listed below and then discussed in turn.

- The process of implementation revealed things that needed to alter.

- Data collected through testing made it possible to focus on particular subjects, particularly literacy and numeracy.

- The Literacy and Numeracy Strategies at Key Stage 2.

- The Key Stage 3 Strategy.

- Public perceptions of the behaviour or attainment of some groups of young people have led to modifications to the subjects taught in schools.

- Changes in policy at national level resulted in new organisational structures and arrangements.

You might find it helpful to hold in your mind the idea of *instigators* of change and *implementers* of change. In the case of the National Curriculum, the instigators of change are the government, and the implementers are your colleagues in schools.

In this section you will consider the reasons why some particular developments to the curriculum have taken place, and what the government hopes will be achieved in the years up to 2006.

THE PROCESS OF IMPLEMENTATION REVEALED THINGS THAT NEEDED TO ALTER

The National Curriculum was, arguably, implemented as a means of taking control of schools. It was, and remains a very ambitious programme. The original intention was to test all children in all subjects at the end of every key stage. However, it was soon obvious that this was not manageable and there were several almost immediate alterations. When the first cohort of children reached the end of Key Stage 1 in England, testing was limited to core subjects only: mathematics, English and science. At the other end of the age range, Key Stage 4 became congruent with GCSE and pupils took one set of examinations: their GCSEs. Fresh alterations continue to be made to the testing arrangements; these are published in documents that arrive in schools, and on the web.

▶ACTIVITY 8.4

Ask the coordinator or head of department in one of the core subjects to explain to you what is different about this year's SATs to last year's. How does this affect the pupils you support?

◼ DATA COLLECTED THROUGH TESTING MADE IT POSSIBLE TO FOCUS ON PARTICULAR SUBJECTS

The testing of children gathers more and more data over time, so it was not long before there was such a lot of data that it was theoretically possible to compare children and schools from year to year, to check that schools continued to teach the curriculum effectively. It also became possible to track the progress of individuals throughout their schooling, and to note whether progress was maintained.

Because of the huge numbers of pupils involved, it is now possible to predict statistically the *proportion* of an age group that will gain particular results at the end of the next key stage, based on results from the previous one. Schools extrapolate this process to predict GCSE grades of pupils on the basis of their Key Stage 3 results, and sometimes even Key Stage 2 results, under the assumption that it is possible to make accurate predictions about individuals' future examination success. Although these results may give some indication as to a pupil's likely future examination performance, it is not possible to see into the future of a particular person, whether you use statistics or a crystal ball.

What is possible is to monitor a particular pupil against the expectations for a group of similar pupils of the same age and same previous attainment, and if the pupil appears to be underachieving, to ask questions why this might be. Undoubtedly this monitoring has helped in the overall recent apparent improvement in pupil performance. The downside is that the process generates considerable time-consuming work for teachers, particularly in planning for, and keeping records of, individuals' past and projected attainment, which many would argue is at the expense of actually teaching. The big question is whether improvement in end-of-key stage tests really indicates improved learning or whether pupils and teachers are better prepared for the data-gathering process in which they are inevitably entangled.

▉ LITERACY AND NUMERACY STRATEGIES AT KEY STAGE 2

Competence in literacy and numeracy seem to be an increasing problem for adults, not just in Britain, but in much of the developed world (NCES, 1995). Unemployment is associated with poor literacy and numeracy skills, and at the other end of the scale, research shows us that graduates with A-level mathematics are likely to earn significantly more than those without A-level mathematics (Dolton and Vignoles, 1999).

Driven by a focus on raising standards in literacy and numeracy, in 1998 the government decided on a further huge national initiative which tried to link success in tests with the *manner* in which teaching was done, i.e. the pedagogy. At Key Stage 2, targets were set for schools in mathematics, science and English, and the Literacy and Numeracy Strategies were introduced. Children's attainment in associated tests has risen since the introduction of the strategies – teaching to the test, as many commentators began to call the primary school curriculum. Government targets for Key Stage 2 are set out in Figure 8.2. There is little or no evidence that the whole class interactive teaching promoted by the strategies is any more effective *per se* than other pedagogies used by effective teachers. Indeed, the biggest rise in test scores has been in primary science even though science comes without a tight prescription of teaching (Torrance, 2002). Nevertheless, the strategies do provide help for non-specialist teachers, a focus for planning lessons, resource materials, and a network of advisory staff whose job is to help spread consistent practice across the schools in each local education authority.

- Raise standards in English and mathematics so that by 2004, 85% of 11-year-olds achieve level 4 or above and 35% achieve level 5 or above with this level of performance sustained to 2006.

- Ensure that by 2006, the number of schools in which fewer than 65% of 11-year-olds achieve level 4 or above in English and mathematics is significantly reduced.

- Reduce to zero the number of local education authorities where fewer than 78% of 11-year-olds achieve level 4 or above in 2004, thus narrowing the attainment gap.

(DfES, 2002: 9)

8.2   TARGETS FOR KEY STAGE 2, ENGLAND, 2002–6

▉ THE KEY STAGE 3 STRATEGY

The Key Stage 3 Strategy extends beyond English and mathematics to include science and foundation subjects as well. Key Stage 3 is a transition period, where knowledge, skills and understanding developed in the primary years are built on to provide secure foundations for work at Key Stage 4. Data from National Curriculum tests confirms what teachers and parents already know: that particular groups of pupils in general fail to consolidate their learning in this key stage, with commensurate poor performance at GCSE. Specifically, progress in English, mathematics and science has been disappointing overall, as well as showing that under-performance is particularly noticeable for boys, and for certain groups of ethnic minority students, e.g. from the Caribbean, or Pakistan, in each case with boys under-performing in relation to girls and class remaining a significant factor.

The Key Stage 3 strategy was introduced in 2001 specifically to address the problems of performance in the eleven-to-fourteen age range. Figure 8.3 shows the government targets. These are basically simple: build on the strength of Key Stage 2. Take each pupil from level four in maths, science and English at age eleven to level five at age fourteen, and the prospect of GCSE grade C or above becomes very likely (90 per cent). Beginning with mathematics and literacy, the strategy has extended to include science, ICT, thinking skills and foundation subjects. As it is very important for eleven- to fourteen-year-olds to develop their thinking skills across the entire curriculum in preparation for their increasing academic and social independence, there is a big emphasis on linking knowledge and skill, particularly in literacy and numeracy, across the whole curriculum.

- By 2004, 75% of 14-year-olds achieve level 5 or above in English, mathematics, and ICT (70% in science) nationally, and by 2007, 85% (80% in science).

- By 2004, as a minimum performance target, at least 65% of 14-year-olds to achieve level 5 and above in English and mathematics, and 60% in science in each local education authority.

- By 2004, no more than 15% of 14-year-olds will fail to attain at least one level 5.

- By 2007, the number of schools where fewer than 60% of 14-year-olds achieve level 5 or above in English, mathematics and ICT is significantly reduced.

- By 2007, 90% of pupils reach level 4 in English and mathematics by age 12.

(DfES, 2002: 10)

8.3   TARGETS FOR KEY STAGE 3, ENGLAND, 2002–6

This dependence on national teaching strategies to achieve improvement is very optimistic. However, it disregards characteristics both of pupils and of learning that many educators believe to be important. For example, it has been demonstrated in the UK and in other countries that family

---

► ACTIVITY 8.5

Open the Standards website, http://www.standards.dfes.gov.uk/keystage3

Click on one of the subjects you support. Browse the site, and see if you can find:

- advice about supporting English and mathematics in your subject
- advice provided about the potential for teaching assistants to support the subject.

---

background and career expectation are associated with pupils' performance at school. Evidence suggests that both boys and girls from middle-class families are more likely to achieve highly in tests (e.g. Cooper and Dunne, 1999), and this is borne out by the differential data on pupils from ethnic minorities. For instance, boys from Pakistani British families do significantly worse at school than boys from Indian British families; this correlates exactly with the socio-economic position of Pakistani British and Indian British people in England (DfES, 2001), and suggests that economic factors are more influential than ethnicity alone.

Not only is attainment differentiated by socio-economic grouping, evidence suggests that learning of literacy and numeracy takes place significantly in the setting in which it is applied. Consequently, there is a responsibility for employers to develop the literacy and numeracy skills of their employees, following on from the preparation in school. Such challenges indicate that there may be issues that large-scale national strategies will have difficulty coping with.

Four general principles outline the overall aims of the strategy for Key Stage 3. They are as follows:

- *Expectations:* Raise expectations of high achievement, both teachers' expectations, and most importantly, pupil expectations of themselves.

- *Progression:* Ensure that pupils build on what they have already learned. This means that pupils do not get an academic 'fresh start' when they arrive at a new key stage even if this coincides with starting a new school (as is often the case at the beginning of Key Stage 3). In such cases it is the responsibility of the schools to share information about the pupils' performance in relation to the National Curriculum, so as to provide the pupils with a challenging programme of study from the start. When pupils do change schools, it cannot be emphasised enough that it takes some time, often several months, to settle down, and it is often quite difficult for teachers to gain a thorough understanding of the students' all-round capabilities.

- *Engagement:* Young people learn best when they are interested and motivated to work. This strand seeks to support teachers in teaching in ways that maximise the time the pupils spend doing activities that will help them to learn.

- *Transformation:* The aim is to strengthen teaching and learning in schools so that all pupils can achieve the highest level of which they are capable. This means a national programme of professional development for teachers, complemented by a whole host of monitoring techniques (Ofsted, data comparisons, threshold standards, etc.) to check that teachers are 'benefiting' from this support and that pupils are learning more.

▶ ACTIVITY 8.6

Try to observe an English lesson and a mathematics lesson. How are the lessons structured? You will probably notice a lively interactive starter, some whole class teaching, and some group tasks, ending up with a round-up or plenary session. This lesson structure is the one advised by the strategies at Key Stages 2 and 3.

PUBLIC PERCEPTIONS OF THE BEHAVIOUR OR ATTAINMENT OF SOME GROUPS OF YOUNG PEOPLE HAS LED TO MODIFICATIONS MADE TO THE SUBJECTS TAUGHT IN SCHOOLS

The National Curriculum in England has extended recently to include citizenship at Key Stages 3 and 4. In Wales, citizenship education is covered by the community aspect of personal and social education (PSE) and from 2003, PSE will become a statutory element within the basic curriculum. There is also an increasing emphasis on the place of physical activity. A discussion of why citizenship has been introduced into the curriculum is beyond the scope of this book. Here we just draw attention to two events and circumstances during the mid–late 1990s, which motivated the government to take action. First, the murder in 1993 of Stephen Lawrence, a black schoolboy, and the subsequent MacPherson Inquiry pointed to inherent racism in national institutions, notably the police. Second, there was very poor turnout by the electorate for local and government elections, contrasting significantly with large polls for popular TV competitions, e.g. *Big Brother, Pop Idol*, at a time of challenging social, political, scientific and cultural issues such as global warming, religious fundamentalism and political asylum.

- Enhance the take-up of sporting opportunities by 5- to 16-year-olds by increasing the percentage of schoolchildren who spend a minimum of two hours each week on high-quality PE and school sport within and beyond the curriculum from 25% in 2002 to 75% by 2006 (joint target with the Department for Culture, Media and Sport).

- By 2005–6, ensure that every secondary school can offer five days enterprise activity to pupils.

(DfES, 2002: 11)

8.4   TARGETS FOR SPORT AND FOR ENTERPRISE ACTIVITY, 2002–6

Figure 8.4 shows the targets for improving the general well-being of school pupils, and their preparation for making a contribution to the economy. The emphasis on physical education is as a result of increasing evidence of obesity and unfitness on the part of young people, leading to health problems in later life such as heart disease and strokes, and costing the health service a considerable amount of money. Medical advice suggests good habits of diet and recreation early on can forestall some of the most debilitating conditions. The physical education targets are a deliberate attempt to improve the health of young people, and to link exercise also to personal, social and health education (PSHE), through which, among other things, pupils are taught about the importance of diet, misuse of drugs and alcohol, the importance of regular exercise, etc.

■ CHANGES IN POLICY AT NATIONAL LEVEL LEAD TO NEW ORGANISATIONAL STRUCTURES AND ARRANGEMENTS

Reflecting on this chapter so far, it is clear that it would not be possible for a national curriculum to stay fixed for long without becoming out of date. The circumstances in which we live and in which young people are being prepared for adulthood are changing rapidly and continuously.

Data collected about pupils' and schools' performance has led to the strategies for teaching and learning at Key Stages 2 and 3, and the next focus is to be on fourteen- to nineteen-year-olds (which will include Key Stage 4). The professional development programmes for teachers, head teachers and governors continue to raise issues about government policies, as a result of which development continues. Serious questions are now being articulated about the effects on pupils and teachers of continued pressure to perform.

One new development is the recognition of the activities of teaching assistants in supporting teaching and learning, through the development of standards for higher-level teaching assistants. This will involve professional recognition for teaching assistants working at a high level in schools, together with a clear career progression opportunity. This is a very radical proposal and is hotly debated currently. Figure 8.5 shows an extract from a discussion on the government Standards website discussion forum, http://www.standards.dfes.gov.uk/forums.

> I am also a secondary mathematics teacher. I teach a lot of low ability classes and without the help and support of the LSAs who work with me, my job would be twenty times harder. I sometimes work with a learning support teacher and we work together to deliver the lesson. Should we not be looking at what is best for the kids and how they can get the most from the talents and skills of all the adults working with them in the classroom and stop being snobby about being a teacher?

8.5   FROM THE STANDARDS WEBSITE DISCUSSION FORUM

The professional development of teaching assistants is discussed in depth in Chapters 11 and 12, as it is perhaps one of the most significant structural reorganisations emerging from the government's determination to raise standards.

REFERENCES

Chitty, C. and Dunford, J. (1999) *State Schools – New Labour and the Conservative Legacy.* Woburn: Worburn Press

Cooper, B. and Dunne, M. (1999) *Assessing Children's Mathematical Knowledge: Social class, sex and problem-solving.* Buckingham: Open University Press.

DfEE/QCA (1999) *The National Curriculum (England).* London: HMSO, and online at http://www.nc.uk.org

DfES (2001b) *Youth Cohort Study: The activities and experiences of 19-year-olds: England and Wales 2000 Reference ID SFR43/2001*. London: DfES

Dolton, P. and Vignoles A. (1999) *The Labour Market Returns to Different Types of Secondary School Curricula*. Paper presented at the Royal Economic Society's 1999 Annual Conference at the University of Nottingham.

MacPherson of Cluny, Sir W., advised by Cook, T., Sentamu, J. and Stone, R. (1999) *The Stephen Lawrence Inquiry*. Report of an inquiry presented to Parliament by the Secretary of State for the Home Department. London: The Stationery Office, February 1999.

NCES (1995) *Literacy, Economy and Society: Results from the International Adult Literacy Survey*. Washington: National Center for Education Statistics.

The National Assembly for Wales / ACCAC (2000) *The National Curriculum in Wales*. Cardiff: ACCAC, and online at http://www.accac.org.uk

Torrance, H. (2002) *Can Testing Really Raise Educational Standards?* Professorial lecture, 11 June 2002, University of Sussex.

CHAPTER 9

Inclusion: do we know what we mean?

'Inclusion' is a word you will have heard many times. Many people talk about inclusion and we all tend to think we know what it means. But do we, and do we all understand and mean the same when we use the term? In this chapter you will be encouraged to question more critically what the term inclusion means – for you, for the pupils you work with, for teachers and for parents.

During your study in higher education you will come across many terms and concepts about which you will be required to think critically. Sometimes these terms will be new to you; sometimes they will be terms whose meanings may have become relatively 'taken for granted', such as 'ability' or 'progress'. The aim of this chapter is to take a specific area with which you are likely to be fairly familiar, and unpack some of the complexity that underpins it. When you do this with a term or concept, you will never think of it in the same way again. This is part of the fascination of learning in higher education – the way your thinking develops.

Topics covered in this chapter include:

- Thinking about inclusion.
- Inclusion and special educational needs.
- The challenge of inclusion.
- Expanding the concept of inclusion.

THINKING ABOUT INCLUSION

The starting point in this chapter is to explore what you and other teaching assistants understand by the term 'inclusion'.

▶ ACTIVITY 9.1

Take a few minutes now to think about the following questions. Jot down your ideas.

- What does the term 'inclusion' mean to you?
- Now think about inclusion in relation to your school. How inclusive do you think your school is? Why do you think this? What is it about your school that influences how inclusive you think it is?

If you are working with other teaching assistants, you might like to share your ideas with colleagues. Are there similarities between your thinking and that of your colleagues? Are there any differences? Why do you think this is?

Have a look now at Figure 9.1, which contains a set of statements about inclusion, written by a group of teaching assistants. You may find that some of their thoughts are similar to your own. There are a number of issues that these teaching assistants raise and some of them are highlighted below:

- When thinking about inclusion, several teaching assistants focus on disabled pupils or those with special educational needs.

- Others focus on issues surrounding learning, for example, the right to learn in effective groups (Gary), pupils working at their own level (Sara) or pupils enjoying learning and experiencing individual successes (Tony).

- Some statements highlight more diverse learning needs, such as ethnic and cultural diversity, gender, disability, age and behaviour problems (Mary).

- Other teaching assistants emphasise the social and relational aspects of inclusion. Gary, for instance, voices concerns about relationships and Roxy comments on opportunities for social mixing.

■ Lastly, there are thoughts about inclusion being concerned with the prevention of exclusions.

We will return to these teaching assistants' comments again later in this chapter. However, what should be becoming clear is that inclusion is not a simple concept and it may mean different things to different people.

Roxy:	To allow any child, no matter what their disabilities are, to be allowed to attend a mainstream school, whether they be physical, behavioural, medical or learning difficulties. To be viewed as equal to all pupils. To have the opportunity to mix with children their own age on an equal level.
Gary:	Pupils should have a right to learn in an effective learning group. Any pupil who is removed from a teaching group should be allowed to maintain their own learning. A strategy to repair and rebuild relationships should be put into practice.
Sara:	My understanding of inclusion is that ... the child should be working at their own level and have the appropriate work set for them whether they are working in the main class, small groups, or on their own with a TA. Sadly this is often not the case.
Mary:	Inclusion is giving every child the right to education in mainstream school. All pupils regardless of race, gender, disabilities, cultural differences, age, as well as behavioural problems. The impact on schools is wide and needs to be addressed by government by more funding and training for teachers and teaching assistants, as many more are needed so all children can be accommodated.
Tony:	The opportunity for all students, regardless of their academic or physical ability, to fulfil their individual potential beyond their own expectations. To enable them to take pleasure in learning and their individual successes.
Kirsty:	Inclusion means – 'Include me'. It's about belonging – both educationally and socially
Judi:	Everyone being included in the same environment with the same opportunities to achieve the same goal.
Anna:	Inclusion is the right for all pupils to access the curriculum, and provide them with both experiences and learning opportunities within the school community.

9.1 SOME THOUGHTS ON INCLUSION BY A GROUP OF TEACHING ASSISTANTS

INCLUSION AND SPECIAL EDUCATIONAL NEEDS

When we start to think about inclusion in schools, sometimes the first things that come to mind are special educational needs, learning difficulties or disabilities. Some of the teaching assistants quoted in Figure

9.1 thought about inclusion in this way. Why do you think this is? Our understanding of inclusion has developed over time, but it was perhaps work with pupils who experienced difficulties in learning that initially influenced thinking about inclusion and educational practices the most.

▶ ACTIVITY 9.2

Have a look at the quotations in Figure 9.2 below. When do you think they were written? For each quotation, write down the year you think they come from. Answers can be found at the end of this chapter.

Quotation A:
Experience showed that children put into such [special] classes seldom continued over a period of years to make such progress as would justify their segregation from the rest of the school.

Quotation B:
In recent times there has been a tendency to explore the possibility and potential advantages of forming classes within certain ordinary primary schools for some of the children whose disability is not of the severest and for whom the need for specialised teaching may not preclude their mixing in a normal school community.

Quotation C:
A great many of the children now in special schools or receiving some kind of special education were at one time being taught under ordinary conditions, and the detection of their need was due to the perception of ordinary class-teachers.

Quotation D:
Integration is not simply a new form of provision, another option as it were. It is a process rather whereby the education offered by ordinary schools becomes more differentiated and geared to meeting a wider range of pupil needs.

Quotation E:
Schools should not automatically assume that children's learning difficulties always result solely or even mainly from problems within the child. The school's practices can make a difference – for good or ill.

9.2   WHEN DO YOU THINK THESE QUOTATIONS WERE WRITTEN? CAN YOU DATE THEM?

Of course there is a danger in taking quotations out of context. None are totally reflective of the thinking of their time, but they do serve to help us question some of the thinking that was going on. For instance, you may have been surprised to find that Quotation A was from a text written in 1937 – thinking about including pupils is certainly not new! Or is it? What do you think?

What else can we learn by looking at these quotations?

■ We can see how thinking has moved from a focus on the child to one where the school is recognised as playing a part. For instance, Quotations A (1937), B (1959) and E (1994) are all taken from UK or English government publications. By 1994, the practice of the school was being highlighted as important. It is now known that schools can make a difference and some schools are better than others at including pupils with diverse needs. But before we came to understand that schools can play a part in inclusion, we saw problems as largely (or even solely) attributable to the child.

■ From Quotation C it can also be seen how at that time (1969), as today, there was an emphasis on the import-ance of the identification of pupils' needs. The difference however, was that identification of special needs at that time tended to result in segregation of some kind, usually to a special school, or sometimes to a special class or unit. Quotations C (1969) and D (1981) actually span a significant time in special education, where increasing segregation had led to a review of what was happening. This review was reported in the Warnock Report (1978). The subsequent 1981 Education Act gained the reputation of helping to halt segregation and promoting the integra-tion of pupils with special educational needs into main-stream schools.

■ Quotation B (1959) makes us think about what we mean by normal. What do you think a 'normal school commu-nity' would have looked like in 1959? Do you think there would have been such a thing? The problem with words such as 'normal' is that what may be normal to one person or in one context or time, may not be normal to other people or in other contexts or times. If we think about this in relation to Quotation D (1981), which talks about the recognition of a wider range of pupil needs, we see moves to making diversity the norm in our schools.

There is evidence that people have been thinking about integration or inclusion in different ways for a long time in relation to pupils who experience difficulties in learning or who are disabled. What is the problem? What is so difficult about inclusion? Is it difficult, or is it just that it is taking time to understand?

THE CHALLENGE OF INCLUSION

To help us to think about the challenge of inclusion, we will introduce you to Natasha. Her case study illustrates some of the challenges of inclusion (Jacklin, 1996). As the case study unfolds, we pick up several clues about Natasha from the comments made by her mother and one of her teachers.

Natasha was eleven and in Year Seven. She was on the special educational needs register and by the end of the year was 'known' around the school because of both learning and behavioural difficulties. She transferred to a comprehensive school at the start of Year Seven and at first she seemed to be working hard and enjoying school life. During her second term at the comprehensive her behaviour around school deteriorated and she was often in trouble. In some lessons her behaviour was particularly disruptive and she received a lot of detentions, while in other lessons she seemed to get on fairly well. There were two teaching assistants (Mrs Coombes and Mrs Smith) who supported her in different lessons. By the end of her first year at the comprehensive some staff were concerned about her ability to cope at the school and a few were commenting that she 'shouldn't really be here'.

Although all youngsters are different, it is likely that you will have met a pupil like Natasha in your school. What challenges can you identify so far? One of the challenges of inclusion is how we can encompass everyone in the school community. Ask yourself how you, as a teaching assistant, and how your school may have responded to Natasha. Also as you read on, try putting yourself in Natasha's position and ask yourself how you may have reacted if you were her. What is it that makes a pupil who seemed to be enjoying school and work at the start of Year Seven, become so disaffected? Let's look at the perspectives of some of the people involved to try to understand some of what was happening.

One of Natasha's teachers commented:

> Well there's so much to get through nowadays and when you have a Natasha in the class, well, I'm just pleased to have a teaching assistant around too. Mrs Smith usually supports in my lessons, she's really good and Natasha seems to like her so that works out well for all of us.

This teacher's concerns lie with the amount of work she feels she has to 'get through' and here lies another challenge. How can we ensure our schools are inclusive communities when they are within educational contexts that include such things as league tables which put pressure on teachers to 'get through' the work to ensure pupils achieve highly?

In this teacher's lessons, Natasha is not really any problem when Mrs Smith is there, but the teacher recognises it may be different without the support she provides. The teacher and Mrs Smith have developed effective working relationships and other pupils also benefit from the support she can give to them. From Natasha's teacher's perspective, having a teaching assistant around is really important. What does Natasha think? She had two teaching assistants, each of whom approached support in very different ways.

When Natasha was asked what she thought about school, she said:

> Well I didn't get a good score in the exams; I got the lowest score out of all the year, but, well, I done my best, and yeah, I did get some help in lessons, there was Mrs Coombes, *well*, it was *so* embarrassing, I used to *hate* it, but I liked Mrs Smith because she used to help the others too.

It is interesting that Natasha's first comment was about having the lowest score in the whole year, despite having done her best. It is not difficult to imagine how we would feel in Natasha's place. It is also not difficult to understand the effect this would have had on her self-image and self-esteem. Here inclusion presents us with other challenges: do we value the contributions of all pupils to the life of our schools? How do we do this and how do we show it?

The second point Natasha makes is about the support she had from the two teaching assistants, one she liked and whose support she accepted, the other she rejected as '*so* embarrassing'. The challenge here is not the issue of the support being available, although this was clearly important; it is the way in which the support was given which was more important.

As a teaching assistant, you have an important role to play in relation to the challenges that are highlighted by Natasha's comments. For instance, through being sensitive to pupils' needs, you can be proactive in identifying and highlighting pupils' strengths. In addition, because you tend to spend a lot of time with the same pupils and get to know them well, you are in a position to help identify practices that are effective with particular pupils and discuss these with colleagues. Can you identify other ways in which your role is important in relation to pupils like Natasha?

When thinking about the challenge of inclusion, it is helpful to consider the viewpoints of as many people as possible. For example, Natasha's mother had an interesting perspective. She explained what she felt had happened during Year Seven that had contributed to problems which arose:

> She's [Natasha's] very naïve, and how do you help them with that? The
> trouble is, she's a trusting and gullible child and not street-wise so she gets
> taken in. She's gone for the ruffians up there at the comprehensive, you
> know, as her friends, because she wants accepting and if she can't get it
> somewhere, she'll get it there. At first they'd say 'Go away, you're thick' so
> she started acting big, but she's not crafty like them so she's singled out as
> being disruptive.

From these comments, we begin to get a picture of the way in which
Natasha changed over the year, but more importantly, why she changed.
Having received the lowest score of all the year group in the exams, despite
having done her best, Natasha looked elsewhere for approval and success.
Not being quick enough, or 'crafty' as her mother put it, to get away with
things, she was often caught out. Her reputation in school grew, especially
among some staff – but importantly, not all staff. Why do teachers and
teaching assistants find pupils like Natasha particularly challenging? One
explanation is that the job of teachers and teaching assistants is to ensure
that pupils learn and also that they behave themselves. Therefore,
youngsters such as Natasha challenge our *raison d'être*. They neither behave
as we want (or need) them to behave, nor do they seem to learn what we
teach them. But does it need to be like this? We can see from Natasha's
teacher's comment above that it does not.

Alison, the teaching assistant from Chapter 2, explains that:

> With the special needs students, what I find is that if a child will accept the
> fact that they are on the special needs register and they accept the help they
> are given, then that works well, but some children see it as a stigma and
> don't like anyone trying to help them as they know they are going to be seen
> as stupid by the other children. This can cause problems, so what I do is,
> when I'm working with a child, I try not to sit with them for the whole
> lesson, but help others as well, so the child doesn't feel too stigmatised.

From Alison's perspective it is understandably a lot easier if pupils such
as Natasha accept the help of teaching assistants, but we can see from
Natasha's comments some of the reasons why she may not wish to accept
help in the way it is given. Alison has found a solution to this in her
school and managed to include some pupils through the approach she has
adopted. As Alison pointed out, what might appear to be the easiest
solution is not necessarily the best.

There are lots of things we can learn from Natasha and her experiences
and we have only touched on a few of the challenges of inclusion here.
Take a few minutes now to reflect on the following questions.

► ACTIVITY 9.3

Think about pupils you work with or some that you know around school.

- Do they always behave in the same way? Think about situations in which they behave well and/or enjoy and get on well with their work. Can you also think of situations where this doesn't happen?
- Make a list of the different situations and then, when you have your list, make a second list of the differences between the situations. Can you identify any specific factors about the situations that affect the pupil and his/her behaviour and learning?

In answering the final question in Activity 9.3, it is likely that you will have included some of the following:

- *The peer group*: Friends and other pupils in the peer group are very important to youngsters. As we saw with Natasha, she changed the way she behaved to get their approval. Teaching assistants can make a great deal of difference when supporting in the classroom just by considering such things as pupil groupings or the pupil's self-image among their peers.

- *Attitudes*: People's attitudes are also very important in-fluences on a range of aspects (e.g. a positive attitude towards pupils and believing in them can be a powerful influence on their behaviour and learning). Mrs Smith wanted Natasha to succeed and was keen to find a way of supporting her and the teacher. She understood Natasha's need to maintain her 'street-cred' and the need to find appropriate ways of providing support. She managed this well and was appreciated by both Natasha and the teacher. This is another way in which you can make a real difference in the classroom. You are likely to be a very significant and influential person in the pupil's life.

- *Feeling valued and recognising achievements*. Natasha worked hard but was 'rewarded' with having the lowest score in the year, made known to all. It is perhaps totally unsur-prising that she reacted as she did. In the lessons where her achievements were recognised, she felt good about what she could do. Here again, teaching assistants can be

> so important: just conveying that you believe in the pupil can be so powerful.

This short case study illustrates some of the challenges of inclusion. What other challenges can you identify? Are there perhaps some challenges that are particularly pertinent for your role and your school? Each individual, as well as school communities as a whole, can make a difference in relation to who is 'included' and who is not.

EXPANDING THE CONCEPT OF INCLUSION

So what do we mean when we use the term inclusion? Inclusion is not just about pupils who experience difficulties in learning or who are disabled. It is far more than this. As soon as we start to consider inclusive schooling, we find ourselves considering issues such as rights, equality of opportunity, equity issues, social justice and many others. As you engage with some of the ideas and questions in this section, we hope that it stimulates you to debate and to further reading.

If you read some of Tony Booth's work (see for example, Booth *et al.*, 2002), you will find that he defines inclusive education as the process of increasing the participation of learners within curricula, cultures and communities. This is a very useful way of thinking about inclusion and there are some important ideas here to reflect on. For instance, processes of increasing participation are central to your work as a teaching assistant. This was clearly illustrated in Natasha's case study.

In your school there should be a copy of the *Index for Inclusion*. This resource was distributed free of charge to all schools in England and Wales in 2000. In the *Index* another helpful way of thinking about inclusion has been developed. In addition to evolving inclusive practices (as Alison was doing), and producing inclusive policies (as Alison's school was doing), there is a third dimension, that of developing *inclusive cultures*.

An institutional culture may perhaps be best understood as 'the way we do things around here'. It can be used in relation to the school as a whole (the school culture) but there are usually a range of sub-cultures within this (e.g. pupil cultures, teacher cultures; sometimes departments within secondary schools have their own cultures, as do groups of people who work together, such as in a learning support unit). Use these ideas to think about your school and its sub-cultures in relation to inclusion. It is sometimes helpful to focus on specific examples. For instance, how does your school (and its sub-cultures) value the achievements of pupils like Natasha? You are likely to notice that cultures differ and some are more inclusive than others.

When we think about inclusion, the *Index* suggests we need to think about our practices, policies and cultures. But who are we including? Who are we considering when we think about our policies and practices? Look again at Figure 9.1 and read Kirsty's, Judi's and Anna's statements. They make interesting points. For Kirsty, inclusion is about belonging, both educationally and socially. Judi highlights 'everyone' and Anna relates inclusion to the school community.

▶ACTIVITY 9.4

- Who do you think Judi meant by 'everyone'? Why do you think Kirsty's concept of belonging might be useful when discussing inclusion? Think about their points in relation to Natasha. Do you think she felt she 'belonged', either educationally or socially? Try thinking about these questions and ideas in relation other pupils that you know or work with. Do you think they would feel they belonged?
- At another level, we can focus on the school itself. Think about your school community: who is part of it and who do you think feels part of it (these may be two different things)? Does it reflect the local community, or only part of the local community?

There are a lot of questions to think about here. As we begin to engage with these sorts of ideas, we are challenged to widen our understanding of inclusion. For instance, concepts of 'belonging' and 'school communities' help us to expand the concept of inclusion and to consider diversity more broadly. This has become more evident in the National Curriculum in England, which is underpinned by three principles in relation to inclusion. (These are outlined below; see also pages 32–9 in the National Curriculum handbook for secondary teachers, and pages 30–7 in the National Curriculum handbook for primary teachers, or visit the website www.nc.net).

The first principle highlights the need for learning to be challenging but carefully differentiated so that all pupils can experience success and also achieve their full potential. What can be highlighted here is that this applies to *all* pupils, whatever their attainment. We need to think about inclusion in relation to pupils who are very able, not just those with special educational needs.

The second principle highlights the importance of responding to pupils' diverse learning needs. Again this is seen to encompass *all* pupils: boys and girls from different social, cultural and linguistic backgrounds; those from diverse ethnic groups (including travellers, refugees and asylum seekers); as well as pupils with special educational needs or who are disabled. The concept of diverse learning needs also includes interests, strengths and experiences. Essentially, inclusion in this context is about everyone in our communities.

The third principle highlights the importance of overcoming potential barriers to learning. These may occur in relation to a minority of pupils who have particular needs, generally those with special educational needs, those who are disabled, or those for whom English is an additional language. Thinking about potential barriers to learning is useful conceptually, as it helps us move beyond 'within-child' factors to other possible factors (and interaction of factors) such as the policies, practices and cultures of our schools. For instance, in Natasha's case study, the concept helps us move beyond 'Natasha's problem' to considering factors such as the way support was given in lessons.

In this chapter we have begun to explore some aspects of inclusion but in reality we have only just started to touch the surface. Earlier we noted that schools themselves can make a difference to inclusion (e.g. Figure 9.2, Quotation E). In addition we can see from the example of Natasha that individual teachers and teaching assistants can also make a difference. Although only a relatively minor adjustment, Mrs Smith's strategy was a powerful one in helping Natasha feel that she belonged. Alison's strategy of 'helping the others too' is also a small, but effective strategy. Sometimes it is the small things that can make a real difference, that can really increase the participation of learners in the curricula, cultures and communities of our schools. The seemingly small things *do* make a difference. *You* can really make a difference.

REFERENCES

Booth, T., Ainscow, M., Black-Hawkins, K., Vaughan, M. and Shaw, L. (2002) *Index for Inclusion: Developing learning and participation in schools*, 2nd edn. Bristol: CSIE. (1st edn, 2000).

DfEE/QCA (1999) *The National Curriculum (England)*. London: HMSO.

DES (1978) *Special Educational Need* (Report of the Warnock Committee). London: HMSO.

Jacklin, A. (1996) *The Transfer Process Between Special and Mainstream Schools*. Unpublished DPhil Thesis, University of Sussex.

ANSWERS TO ACTIVITY 9.2

Quotation A: 1937

Board of Education (1937) *Handbook of Suggestions for the Consideration of Teachers and Others Concerned in the Work of Public Elementary Schools*. London: HMSO: page 35.

Quotation B: 1959

HMI (1959) *Primary Education: Suggestions for the consideration of teachers and others concerned with the work of primary schools*. London: HMSO: page 109.

Quotation C: 1969

Jackson, S. (1969) *Special Education in England and Wales*, 2nd edn. London: Oxford University Press. (1st edn, 1966): page 2.

Quotation D: 1981

Hegarty, S. and Pocklington, K. with Lucas, D. (1981) *Educating Pupils with Special Needs in the Ordinary School*. Windsor: NFER-Nelson: page 1.

Quotation E: 1994

DFE (1994) *Code of Practice on the Identification and Assessment of Special Educational Needs*. London: HMSO, Para 2:19: page 11.

CHAPTER 10

Thinking about behaviour management

Working with pupils whose behaviour is challenging is perhaps one of the most demanding but potentially the most rewarding aspect of school life. Many teaching assistants are employed specifically to work with pupils who present emotional and behavioural difficulties (EBD). Those of you who regularly work with individuals or groups of pupils whose behaviour is considered to be problematic will be able to relate to the experiences of the pupils and teaching assistants in this chapter. Those of you who don't tend to work with these pupils will no doubt be aware of children in your school who present with more challenging behaviour.

Whatever your role and experiences in school, you are all likely to have met with groups or individual pupils who present you with some problems, or who maybe just won't 'play the game'. You are not alone! Most people working in schools have experienced difficulties managing pupil behaviour at some point in their career, even some who may now appear to be so good at it.

Managing behaviour is an integral part of everything we do in schools. However, there is no magic answer to how to manage behaviour successfully – if there was, we would all do it and there would be no more problems. Nevertheless, there are some approaches and ways of working which can help, and that is what this chapter is about.

Topics covered in this chapter include:

- **Understanding why things happen.**
- Catch 'em being good.

- Say what you mean . . . and mean what you say.

- Working with others in school.

UNDERSTANDING WHY THINGS HAPPEN

In your role as a teaching assistant, you may at times be responsible for managing groups of pupils or even whole classes. A good starting point for thinking about managing pupil behaviour is to spend some time trying to understand why pupils may sometimes present us with a challenge. In this section, we will do this by focusing initially on whole class or group management, and particularly on some of the classes or groups with whom you spend more time, before moving on to thinking about individual pupils.

In schools there is an expectation that pupils will both behave and learn. Some would argue that that is what schools are there for. When pupils do both, i.e. they behave and they learn, that's fine, but when they don't . . .! From the point of view of teaching assistants (and teachers too), this challenges us right at the heart of what we are there to do and that is often not easy for us to cope with. After we have spent a little time in the classroom, it is not long before we realise that teaching does not necessarily mean that pupils are learning. Similarly, although we might set out to keep order, we may find ourselves surrounded by chaos. Sometimes it begins to feel as if someone forgot to let the pupils in on what their role in this game is supposed to be! We can end up feeling inadequate. Lesson number one: don't panic, you are not alone. It is important to remember that sometimes what you intend to happen and what actually takes place may not be the same. However, there are a number of approaches that can help you manage pupil behaviour.

▶ ACTIVITY 10.1

Think about the teachers and teaching assistants in your school and choose one that you admire for the way they manage the pupils with whom they work. Picture some of their lessons, or better still watch them in action. It is likely that they will make behaviour management look easy – it isn't, or at least, it needs to be worked at. Jot down thoughts in response to the following questions:

- What is special about their lessons? Why did you choose this person? What do they do that seems to make them good at managing the class or group?

- Now make a list of the qualities that this person seems to have. What is it about them that seems to make them able to manage the class or group?
- If you are able to talk to this person, ask them how they go about managing the class or group. What strategies do they use and why?

Teachers and teaching assistants who manage classes and groups well, often have had a lot of practice. They also expect pupils to behave, and they manage to convey this expectation to the pupils. They do this through their manner, what they say and what they do. Expectations are powerful and if you are nervous at first, then a little acting can help you, i.e. don't let the pupils *see* that you are feeling nervous. Working on developing effective relationships with pupils is an important strategy. They will want you to be fair and up-front; they will also want to feel they can trust you, and that includes being able to trust you to keep order. In addition, although they will like you to be friendly, this does not mean that they want you to be their friend. Getting the balance right is not always easy. Teaching assistants are often in a position where they get to know individual pupils well and pupils may confide in them. Get the relationship right, develop mutual respect, and the pupils will probably end up wanting to please you, and that is a really important factor in managing behaviour.

► ACTIVITY 10.2

For this activity, choose a teacher that you admire for the way they manage the pupils. This time think about (or better still observe) one of their lessons and in particular focus on what happens at the beginning, in the middle and at the end of that lesson. In relation to each stage, think about the following questions:

- What did this teacher actually do and say each time they wanted the pupils to do something (e.g. stop and listen, change activity, clear away, etc.). How did the pupils respond to this?
- How were the stages of the lesson managed: for instance, how were the pupils settled at the start of the lesson?
- List as many different strategies as you can that this teacher used to manage the pupils (e.g. humour, use of voice, etc).
- If possible, discuss your observations with the teacher afterwards.

What you learn from this teacher about managing groups will be helpful to you in your role in school. Pupils tend to respond better to someone (whether teacher or teaching assistant) who is organised, calm, purposeful and generally 'on the ball'. Spending the first few minutes of a lesson hunting for something, organising resources, etc., or generally fiddling around while expecting the pupils to wait, may well result in problems. Be well prepared and well organised – or expect problems. You should be ready to give your attention to the pupils right from the word go. It also helps if you like the subject and the activities you are doing with the pupils, if you are enthusiastic and if (from the pupils' point of view) you are going to be worth listening to. After all, they may well be sitting there deciding whether they are going to be a captive audience for the next half an hour or so . . . or whether they are not!

The teacher whose lesson you observed was likely to have been doing all of this and more. You probably will have identified much more in relation to how they manage groups of pupils than we have noted here. The more you can watch others at work and think about how they do it, the more you will learn. You will also learn a great deal from your own experiences, both when things go well and when things go less well. Just remember, don't get disheartened if things do go wrong – we learn lots from our mistakes. Persevere and it will come right. Talk to colleagues, think about what happened and try to identify:

- what went well and why

- what went wrong and why

- what you will do next time.

Then you too may receive the accolade 'you can manage us quite well now, Miss', as did one teaching assistant who persevered with a group of pupils.

Everything we have discussed so far in relation to managing classes or groups holds good for individual pupils too. You will find it helpful to keep this in mind as we move now from more general class and group management to thinking about individual pupils who may present with more challenging behaviour.

Some teaching assistants are employed in schools to work specifically with pupils who have special educational needs. They may spend a lot of time with particular groups or individual pupils (e.g. in a secondary school where the teaching assistant may support the pupils in a number of subjects). In these cases, teaching assistants are highly likely to be spending more time with some pupils than any other adult in the school. The fund of knowledge built up by the teaching assistant can make a valuable contribution to an understanding of why pupils behave as they do.

Pam, the teaching assistant we met in Chapter 4, recalled how, following a course that she took, she stopped just accepting pupils as 'awkward', and started trying to understand why things were happening. This proved to be extremely important for one particular pupil and Pam's comments are pertinent here too:

> I deal with one particularly disruptive pupil. I've tried talking to him, taking him out of lessons. I'd tried all different ways of trying to get through to him. Then I spoke to his tutor and his head of year about him and the school had him assessed by an Ed Psych and they found he was dyslexic. But a year ago, I wouldn't have looked at him so deeply; if it hadn't been for the university course, I would have just accepted him as an awkward pupil and got on with it, but because I'd been on the course I had the confidence to say something. I didn't know he was dyslexic, but I knew it was worth talking about his behaviour to the head of year, I felt confident to talk to others about him because I now have a better understanding of the pupils and knew something wasn't right.

We saw with Natasha (whom we met in Chapter 9) that there was also a reason that underpinned the way her behaviour had deteriorated during Year Seven. Knowing this, staff were in a better position to make school a more positive experience for her (and for everyone else too) and to modify her behaviour. We identified four main influential factors in Natasha's case:

- difficulties she experienced with the curriculum
- staff attitudes towards this, both positive and negative
- the school culture
- her peer group.

You won't always be able to find a possible reason in the way that Pam did, but trying to see beyond the behaviour and seeing the person first is really important. This is what led to a better understanding of Natasha's difficulties and was the first step in responding to her. Natasha's case demonstrates how it is important to keep in mind that behaviour can vary according to the context and the people involved. In the next section we build on these ideas as we begin to focus more specifically on different approaches to behaviour management.

CATCH 'EM BEING GOOD

You may well have heard this expression before, but even if you haven't, it is worth remembering – and using. 'Catch 'em being good' means just that, consciously looking for times when the pupil is being good and actually catching them doing what they should be doing. This is important because all too often we can find ourselves only ever catching them doing what they shouldn't do, and therefore we always seem to be telling them off. If we can catch pupils being good, we can begin to change our negative interactions to positive ones.

▶ ACTIVITY 10.3

In this activity, we would like you to take a little time to focus on one pupil in your school. Careful observation is important. Choose a pupil for whom you have some concerns in relation to behaviour management.

- Observe them carefully during a lesson, or over part of a day. Do a simple count of how many times other people (staff or pupils) interact with the pupil. Count positive interactions and negative interactions separately (an interaction can be verbal, people talking to the pupil, or it may be non-verbal, such as a frown or a smile or a gesture – count all interactions that occur).
- Now observe the pupil again. This time, when noting positive interactions, also look for where the pupil is behaving or working well – this may be unnoticed by the other adults in the room. Try to record as carefully as possible what happens.

Activity Health Warning: *This task may be more difficult to carry out than it appears. Think carefully about where and how you can observe. You may also find that you observe more than it is possible to record. Don't worry, just do your best and fill in any gaps later.*

When you counted positive and negative interactions, you may have been surprised by the number of negative interactions that occurred. This is not unusual: people are often surprised by this when they take time to watch behaviours that they have come to take for granted.

In the second part of the task, you may have found that interactions tended to be negative while positive behaviours went unnoticed. Unfortunately this happens sometimes when we get so engrossed in the teaching and learning activity that we don't notice the pupils being good. We only notice when they start to do something that upsets the flow of the lesson. It sometimes takes a conscious effort to change what we notice and what we do. For all pupils it is important that we notice them being good, and not just notice when they start to misbehave (we all like to be praised and noticed for what we've done well). However, for pupils whose main interactions are negative, this is even more important. It is this that lies behind the phrase 'Catch 'em being good' – try to ensure that being good is noticed.

In the second part of the task, you may have felt that there were no positive incidents to record. If this is the case, you need to look for smaller incidents. For example, a smaller positive incident may be that the pupil did actually initially sit in their seat, although things went wrong after that (sometimes you only just 'catch them' at first!). Also try looking at different contexts. If we think back to Natasha, when and where do you think we could catch Natasha being good? For Natasha, this tended to be context-specific. There was a difference between lessons. We could easily catch her being good in the lessons described by the teacher (quoted in the previous chapter) and where she was supported by Mrs Smith.

What is important is that we now have a starting point for more positive interactions with the pupil. In the case of some pupils, we have a starting point for convincing them that they can be good. For others we have a starting point for demonstrating to them what constitutes good behaviour (you may be surprised to know that some pupils are no longer really sure what people want from them). We can now begin to break the negative, downward cycle that can happen with some pupils, described in the words of one 12-year-old pupil, Shaun: 'If you step out of line they nag at you and nag at you . . . and in the end you make too many mistakes and you just give up' (Jacklin, 1996). Getting out of this cycle may start with catching them being good and being able to say something positive for a change, rather than 'nag'.

SAY WHAT YOU MEAN . . . AND MEAN WHAT YOU SAY

This is another very useful phrase that it is worth remembering – and again, worth putting into practice. We will look at the two halves of the phrase separately.

■ SAY WHAT YOU MEAN . . .

Empty praise may well be worse than no praise at all. This is why catching them being good is so important. Now you will have something you can genuinely point out as good to praise, or even something that can simply form the basis of a positive interaction, rather than a 'nag'. Pupils need you to be genuine; they need to know and feel secure with you; they need to know where they are and be able to trust you. You need to be able to communicate clearly what you mean. However, in order to be able to say what you mean, you need to start by knowing what it is you do mean.

▶ ACTIVITY 10.4

Look back to Chapter 9 and the description of Natasha. What do you think teachers and teaching assistants may have meant when they said her behaviour 'deteriorated around school', or that she was 'often in trouble', or that her behaviour was 'particularly disruptive', or even that in some lessons she seemed to 'get on fairly well'? If possible, compare your thoughts with those of others. What conclusion do you reach?

Depending on how much time you can give to this activity, you may arrive at quite a long list of possibilities. It is likely that you will have been influenced by pupils that you know and work with and what it might mean in each of their cases. Unfortunately we tend to use vague phrases like 'often in trouble' or 'particularly disruptive' to describe pupils' behaviour in the mistaken assumption that we all know what they mean. It is likely that when you read Natasha's description (in Chapter 9), you conjured up a picture of a pupil based on these assumptions. We all do this, but if we really want to say what we mean, this is no longer good enough.

You will probably have worked out by now that there is only one answer to Activity 10.4. We don't really know what the teacher and teaching assistants meant when they described Natasha's behaviour as having 'deteriorated around school', we can only guess. For each one of the phrases we could list a whole range of possible behaviours but it is not until we take time to sit and observe, as you did in Activity 10.3, that we can begin to identify exactly what the nature of the problem might be. One way to tackle it is to take what is known as a *behavioural approach* (see Figure 10.1) and focus on behaviours that we can actually observe.

Focusing on one pupil again and using your observations from Activity 10.3, try to identify and specify more closely what aspect of the behaviour

There are a number of different theoretical approaches that help us to both understand behaviour and develop strategies to help pupils who present with challenging behaviour. Three important approaches are:

- *Behavioural*, which focuses on observable behaviours, with the aim of increasing desirable behaviour (by positively reinforcing it) and decreasing undesirable behaviours.

- *Cognitive*, which focuses on pupils' perceptions and interpretations (for instance, of themselves or of what happens in particular situations), their self-esteem or how they attribute the causes of their problems.

- *Systemic*, which focuses more on the interactions between different people, their expectations and interpretations of events, or on the interactions between the different perspectives of those involved in events.

(See Ayers, Clarke and Murray (2000) for a more detailed discussion and practical examples of each of these approaches.)

10.1   THEORETICAL APPROACHES TO BEHAVIOUR MANAGEMENT

is causing the problem. (You may need to go back and observe the pupil again – focus carefully on what you see, i.e. focus on observable behaviours.) For instance, does the pupil keep getting out of their seat, or keep calling out? Do they tend to suddenly 'explode', or are they just generally 'loud'; if so, what does this mean? Some people (teachers and teaching assistants) find certain behaviours more difficult to cope with in their lessons than others. This means that in some lessons one aspect of behaviour may be seen to be more of a challenge than in other lessons. A word of warning – don't try to focus on everything (or even several things) at once. Be realistic and be specific. Try also to pick an aspect of behaviour where you will be able to see some progress. Small focused steps are important, especially initially. For instance, if you decide to focus on the 'always getting out of their seat' behaviour, then for now, you may need to ignore the associated 'loudness'.

Once you know what behaviour it is you intend to focus on, then look for when that behaviour occurs and when it does not occur. To do this, you need to observe carefully. For instance, does the pupil actually take a long time to settle so that they spend much of the early part of lessons getting out of their seat, while the latter part of lessons tend to present fewer problems? Or does the reverse happen, perhaps? Do they tend to come into lessons with few problems, but start getting out of their seat later on? Ask yourself whether the behaviour is sparked off by anything in particular.

When making observations of behaviour in this way, an *ABC* (Antecedents, Behaviour, Consequences) analysis can sometimes be useful. This helps us to think about, and focus on: what happened before the incident (the *antecedents*); the *behaviour* itself; and the effects of that behaviour (the *consequences*). Use a table such as the one in Figure 10.2. Start by identifying the behaviour and put that in the middle column. In the example we have here, you would need to do this for several 'gets out of seat' incidents. Then think about what triggered the behaviour (the antecedent), and also what was the consequence of the behaviour (what happened as a result). There could be a number of possible triggers and consequences; for example, other pupils, the work, or perhaps something the teacher said, or an interaction between any of these. Patterns can emerge that you weren't aware of before. This kind of process can be helpful in understanding what is going on and in identifying and targeting desirable and undesirable behaviours.

Antecedents	Behaviour	Consequences
	Got out of seat and went across the room to talk to Ben.	

10.2   AN ABC ANALYSIS

Through this process you might identify that far from always being out of their seat, the pupil is generally in their seat for at least 60 per cent of the time, a positive starting point (although still a way to go). You may also have discovered that the pupil tends to come into lessons with little problem and the wandering around the room tends to come later in the lesson. The ABC analysis may have identified that the more this pupil is out of their seat, the more confrontational they become, but that they tend to leave their seat when they get bored, distracted or in response to other pupils.

In all this, don't forget to involve and talk to the pupil. Natasha's perspective showed that talking to pupils can be extremely helpful. It is also important to establish targets and rewards in consultation with the pupil. In this example, through talking with the pupil you might come up with a target time for them to stay in their seat that they actually feel they can achieve, together with strategies to help them stay on task, and rewards that are meaningful.

If you have thought things through carefully and been specific about the behaviour to be targeted, then you will certainly be able to say what you mean when you communicate with the pupil. However, this may all come to naught if you don't also mean what you say.

■ . . . AND MEAN WHAT YOU SAY

It is important when dealing with any pupils, individually or in groups, that you mean what you say. You need to create clear boundaries and keep to them. To do this you need to be very well aware of school policies, rules, rewards and sanctions. You also need to keep a sense of realism and ensure you have back up should you need it. In particular, you need to ensure that you never promise a reward or threaten a sanction (e.g. a detention) that you don't intend, can't, or won't be able to carry out. Meaning what you say is equally (or perhaps more) important when working with pupils who present with more challenging behaviour.

Having reached the point where you have agreed a behaviour management strategy, it is important to ensure it can all be carried out. Think this through carefully. This kind of approach is time-consuming initially, but well worth the effort – but it does need to be carried through. Don't forget to start the challenge with achievable targets, then step up the targets in manageable and achievable steps. It will be important that the pupil (and you!) can see success.

WORKING WITH OTHERS IN SCHOOL
■

When thinking about behaviour management, don't forget that you are not alone. Not only will you have a range of colleagues within the school, but you are also likely to be working alongside people from a number of other agencies. The more you can work together, pooling ideas, knowledge and understandings, ensuring consistency of approach and so on, the better this will be for the pupil and for yourselves. For pupils who have a statement of special educational need and for those with an individual education plan (IEP) or an individual behaviour plan (IBP), it is important to ensure that strategies and approaches are discussed and agreed with colleagues. Don't try and 'go it alone'.

▶ ACTIVITY 10.5

- Think about your school. How many people do you work with in one day? And over the course of a week? Who do you mostly discuss pupils with?
- Now think about all the other people from different agencies (e.g. the education welfare officer) that you encounter. How many other people are you aware of that come to your school? What are their roles? If you can talk to the special educational needs coordinator at your school, show them your list and see if there are any others that you may have missed.

You will generally find yourself working with many people in schools. Learning to collaborate with other teaching assistants and teachers is not always easy, but ensuring when working together that the relationships are effective can have many benefits. Joan, the teaching assistant we met in Chapter 3, described what happened when there was a feeling among some staff in their school that one teacher was perhaps expecting too much of a pupil whose main behaviour target was to attend school. Joan explains:

> With autistic children you have to give them very strict guidelines about what they have to do, you have to be very organised. The course had given me the confidence to talk to the teacher about how they teach autistic children and what they expect from them. Like I talked to a teacher about one autistic pupil who didn't hand in their homework; the teacher saw this as a problem. Considering what all his other problems were, it wasn't the end of the world – at least this boy was turning up for school, and that was what's important.

Here Joan was working with colleagues to keep focused on the main behavioural target where success was being achieved (attending school each day), while keeping additional targets from clouding the issue until he was ready to tackle them. Good relationships and the confidence she had gained from the course she had taken were important in enabling Joan to broach the problem with the teacher.

One last but very important point in relation to working with others: don't overlook the power of the school culture and of your attitude towards pupils. It is easy to be positive and encouraging when working with pupils who want to learn, who behave well, who smile at you, who pay attention, and so on. It is not so easy when they appear 'switched off', non-communicative, or present with a range of emotional and behavioural difficulties. It your job to engage positively with the pupil from the outset, to persevere, and to look beyond the behaviour to see the person, even when at times you can't understand why things are as they are. Greeting them with a smile so things start positively is important – that may be the first smile they have had for a long time.

Earlier in this chapter we briefly met Shaun, a 12-year-old who transferred to another school before being excluded from his previous school. His experiences may serve to illustrate this point (Jacklin 1996). He came bouncing back from his first visit to the new school looking happier than he had for quite some-time, saying 'He [the head teacher] *wants* me in his school! No-one ever wanted me in their school before.' As we started off by saying, working with pupils whose behaviour is more challenging is perhaps one of the most demanding but potentially the most rewarding aspects of school life.

REFERENCES AND FURTHER READING

Ayers, H., Clarke, D. and Murray, A. (2000) *Perspectives on Behaviour: a practical guide to effective interventions for teachers*, 2nd edn. London: David Fulton. (1st edn, 1995).

Cooper, P., Smith, C.J. and Upton, G. (1994) *Emotional Behaviour Difficulties, Theory to Practice*. London: Routledge.

Cowley, S. (2001) *Getting the Buggers to Behave*. London: Continuum.

Jacklin, A. (1996) *The Transfer Process Between Special and Mainstream Schools*. Unpublished D.Phil Thesis: University of Sussex

Kyriacou, C. (1997) *Effective Teaching in Schools: Theory and practice*, 2nd edn. Cheltenham: Stanley Thornes. (1st edn, 1986).

McNamara, S. and Moreton, G. (2001) *Changing Behaviour: Teaching children with emotional and behavioural difficulties in primary and secondary classrooms*, 2nd edn. London: David Fulton. (1st edn, 1995).

Rogers, B. (2000) *Behaviour Management: a whole school approach*. London: Paul Chapman.

Issues of professionalism

Chapter 11: Finding a place in the professional landscape

In this chapter you will look at the concept of professionalism as it applies in schools and examine how our current conception of the teaching assistant has emerged, looking at key themes that have influenced this. You will then consider some of the possibilities for growth and challenges to the identity of this expanding professional workforce in relation to teachers. Throughout the chapter you are encouraged to evaluate your own position in relation to such issues, and to construct a sense of your own professional expectations.

Chapter 12: Moving on

Ways in which you may wish to develop your career, whether as a higher-level teaching assistant or as a teacher, are examined in this final chapter. Having taken stock of where you are now, the chapter explores some of the options and routes available to you. It aims to enable you to make a more considered and informed decision about 'moving on' and how you may achieve your goal.

CHAPTER 11

Finding a place in the professional landscape

The place of teaching assistants is changing rapidly in schools. Your job description may have become more precise if you are associated with specific activities, such as teaching and learning, or managing behaviour. You may have a supervisor or mentor, who works with you to help you develop your skills. If you are reading this book, you are probably on, or thinking of joining, a training programme. In this chapter we will consider what it is like to be working professionally in schools, and what this might mean in terms of working with others, and in terms of working independently or autonomously.

The following topics are covered in this chapter:

- **Being part of a professional community.** We look at what working professionally in a community means in terms of what teaching assistants do.

- **How teaching assistants have come to be members of the professional community.**

- **Challenges and possibilities in describing the work of teaching assistants.** This section addresses some of the issues that arise as teaching assistants work professionally alongside teachers.

- **Standards, qualifications and performance management.** The chapter concludes by considering briefly the framework of performance management, within which standards and qualifications for continuing professional development for teaching assistants are planned.

BEING PART OF A PROFESSIONAL COMMUNITY

Professions tend to share certain characteristics. The responsibility of a profession to provide the service it offers is taken very seriously, and there are usually strong organisational structures to look after the reputation of the profession and to negotiate on its behalf. This professional association quite often sets out the standards or qualifications that are needed to join, and these are usually high – at least graduate level, often with additional professional qualifications. Normally there is a code of conduct or ethics. The organisation determines what professionals can do and what they are not expected to do, and it may also investigate in the case of complaints. Sometimes the professional association determines how many new entrants to the profession should be admitted, and how often this should be. In other words, members of a profession expect to be self-governing. Professions such as medical doctors, nurses, lawyers and architects have been established for a long time, since the Middle Ages in the case of lawyers! Teaching in England became a fully-fledged profession in 2001 with the setting up of the General Teaching Council for England.

There are also occupations where people work professionally. People working professionally do not necessarily *belong* to a 'profession' in the sense described above. However, they do work in ways that demonstrate adherence to many of the professional characteristics. For instance, they make some day-to-day decisions about what, when and how they do some of their work. People who make their own decisions in this way are working autonomously. Working professionally will include operating autonomously, and taking responsibility if things go wrong. You may not be aware of the decisions you make, as they may seem to be just routine, like putting out the resources for a student that you support. However, some decisions are not routine: they are often complex, but you still make them without apparently thinking for too long. These decisions depend upon your knowledge or understanding of the situation. For example, in Chapter 9, we quote Alison, who said:

> When I'm working with a child, I try not to sit with them for the whole lesson, but help others as well, so the child doesn't feel too stigmatised.

Alison makes a deliberate choice to 'help others as well', based on her experience and her understanding that children who feel stigmatised do not learn as well as those who feel part of a group. This apparently implicit understanding of a situation is called *tacit knowledge* (e.g. Eraut, 1994). Tacit knowledge is always learned through relevant direct practical experience, although the processes by which people gain it can be speeded up through suitable training which prompts people to experiment and to reflect upon ways of doing things. All people working professionally have access to and use considerable tacit knowledge, which is not usually made explicit unless the person is training someone else. Think about a paediatric nurse calculating drug doses for young patients or the airline pilot landing a Jumbo – these people working professionally will get it right without really thinking explicitly what to do each time, even though every move is absolutely critical. When they were learning, though, it was a different matter: each calculation would be carefully checked. Almost everything that experienced and effective teachers do in the classroom is based on tacit knowledge of how the pupils will respond.

▶ ACTIVITY 11.1

Think about your position in your school, and reflect on the different aspects of your work. Can you think of situations where you:

- Contribute to decision-making with colleagues?
- Have control over what you do?

Schools are organisations in which everybody has to make decisions. Some of these, for example the staffing structures or the homework policy, are probably outside the jurisdiction of all except the senior members of staff. However, everyone in the school has a part to play and everyone works professionally in doing so. The decisions made by each and every member of staff are significant in the sense that they impact at least on the school experience of the pupils in the school, and probably on some other adult colleagues as well.

Teaching assistants work closely with individual pupils, and become significant, perhaps sometimes the most significant person, in shaping an individual pupil's learning or behaviour. This is one of the reasons why teachers as well as pupils appreciate the work of teaching assistants in the classroom. One teaching assistant in our study reported considerable pleasure at having been invited to a science department planning meeting, as this showed recognition by the teaching team of the professional job she was doing. Another was delighted when a teacher asked for her to 'move up' with the class when they progressed from Year Seven to Year Eight as this showed that the teacher appreciated how the continuity of support from this individual benefited the pupils' learning; also the teacher probably recognised the benefits of continuing a successful working partnership. The teachers in these examples realised that the teaching assistants have in-depth understanding, often of a different kind, that can help teachers by adding richness to their planning and teaching. Pam was working in such a mutually beneficial professional environment when she said:

> The teachers at the school are brilliant, they let us do basically what we want, and they'll ask our opinion about particular students and even seek advice from us on what should be done about particular students. Sometimes, but not very often, we plan work for students, if the teacher thinks that the work they'll be doing is too difficult for a pupil. This may involve getting work from the Internet.

For the first time, new training standards for teachers insist that trainee teachers learn to 'manage the work of support staff' (DfES, 2002a, 3.3.13: 12). In many schools, demarcations of the roles and responsibilities between teachers and teaching assistants have become well-established and have produced effective partnerships, and, on the whole, teaching assistants are being welcomed as support for teachers. Controversially though, there is some concern from some teachers that managing teaching assistants can add to the workload rather than diminish it; so in some schools this is a cautious welcome. On the other hand, there is recognition by many professional groups that the enhanced support provided – even to the extent sometimes of taking lessons – deserves proper preparation, recognition and status. So far no qualifications are necessary, but training opportunities are being opened up, which will enable some teaching assistants to be recognised as working at a higher level.

Figure 11.1 illustrated how Janet acknowledges that being on a course has enhanced her capabilities at school.

In many respects, Janet is working professionally, as she is acting autonomously and making decisions. She raises the issues of confidence, writing, learning styles, behaviour and motivation, and is clearly reflecting on her practice. Janet, like the other teaching assistants in our study, has a clear picture of what teachers are responsible for: planning and overall delivery of the curriculum; and their own role in relation to this.

It is also evident that that teaching assistants are already being recognised by the teaching profession, but at the time of writing it is not yet clear what sort of organisation will promote the interests of teaching assistants themselves. Teaching unions report that teaching assistants are becoming members as well. Teaching assistants are now joining the community of

I'm teaching now; the course has given me the confidence to do that. It's given me confidence in my own ability, I can now stand in front of a class and feel in control.

I suppose learning about different lesson styles really helped, because I hadn't thought about this before, and I used some of what I'd learned when I was working with a boy in Year 8. This boy has virtually no spelling skills, he spells everything phonetically, and in one lesson he was learning about Shakespeare, and we worked on mapping the characters. It was really interesting to see him do this, and I wouldn't have thought about doing it that way if I hadn't have been taught it at university.

I had a bit of a problem with one boy, not really behaviour problems, but getting him to concentrate; I had to keep bringing him back on task. I used to use his name a lot, and he responded to that. I'd say things like, 'Come on John, let's do this bit here'. I also tried to make the work sound exciting and say, 'We really need to get this done'. I'd sometimes offer to write things down for him because that was what he hated doing, so I'd ask him to tell me what to write and then I'd write it down.

11.1   JANET'S STORY

professionals in schools, and in many ways are developing professional characteristics of their own.

HOW TEACHING ASSISTANTS HAVE COME TO BE MEMBERS OF THE PROFESSIONAL COMMUNITY

It is not long ago that the embarrassing and demeaning term 'Mum's Army' was used to herald this wave of support in schools (the first recorded instance in the on-line archive of the *Times Educational Supplement* was in 1997). The stereotype of women mixing paint and washing up pervaded public discussions about learning support, and teachers were furious at the idea that 'unqualified' people could possibly become responsible for some of their work. In fact increasing numbers of learning support assistants were working to support individual pupils, particularly those with identified special educational needs. These assistants came with various backgrounds and specialist skills, some with A-levels and some graduates.

Joan began as a teaching assistant by supporting a child in primary school, and moved to secondary when the child moved. Several others started as a way of becoming involved with the schools attended by their own children. Few of the teaching assistants we interviewed had qualifications in education and all in the study were most interested to learn more about it. Some wanted to become teachers, recognising that first they would have to complete a degree. Joan was one such person. She said:

The thing that motivated me to do the course was that I'd thought about becoming a teacher and this really was my opportunity to do something about it. Even before I found out about this course, I'd wanted to become a teacher, and there were times when my husband used to say to me, just give the job up and train full time, but that wasn't what I wanted to do; I enjoy my job and I wanted to continue working as a TA (*sic*). I'd always wanted to do something like this. Every year I would get OU (*sic*) stuff and look through the details, but I never got round to doing anything, what with the children and everything, and so it was great when we got the information about the course.

▶ ACTIVITY 11.2

Think about changes to the working practices of teaching assistants that you have seen since you became a teaching assistant.

Increasingly in secondary schools, some teaching assistants work with specific departments in schools, which means that there are opportunities to shift the role from working with individuals to working with groups. This enables teaching assistants to become much more involved in the teaching and learning strategies of the department. However, it has become quite controversial because, by becoming more involved with teaching and learning generally, there is a danger that the boundary of the domain of the professionally qualified teacher becomes compromised.

Teaching assistants are still poorly paid. For some the nature of the work acts to prevent pay increases with experience, because when a pupil leaves school, the teaching assistant starts again with another pupil without past experiences being taken into account. Currently, local agreements are being reached by some education authorities, which should help to establish consistent pay deals, and conditions of work that will include time for planning and other out of classroom work alongside teachers. Without a common pay spine, in some schools, teaching assistants are not able to participate in after-hours activities like planning, because they are paid hourly, and only during the school day. (One of our interviewees, despite ten years experience, was being paid £5.13 per hour.) As Alison describes:

We are the largest department in the school, we have 14 staff and our SEN coordinator is really good, you know. If we are asked to stay after school for a meeting, she will say 'no' because we are not paid for after-school meetings, she really sticks up for us and we are not expected to attend the meetings before school or at any time unless we are actually being paid for being there. We go to the INSET days if they're on a day when we would normally be working, and they are getting better, they do include us now. They have things for our department, whereas at one time we would go to the INSET, but there would be nothing there for us.

At a time of serious teacher shortages, especially in maths and science, additional staff absence puts a lot of pressure on schools for cover. Some teaching assistants do cover whole lessons; they may be paid more for this. This too is also very controversial, as teaching assistants, while knowing the pupils, are not prepared for teaching subjects, and without a framework for becoming trained, do not have the means to become so. However, more than one school is now taking an imaginative approach to the problem of teacher recruitment by employing teaching assistants who *want* to become teachers, and then training them, to graduate level and professional standards, *in situ* (see 'Employment-based routes' in Chapter 12).

We can see growing reliance by schools on teaching assistants to work with pupils in a variety of ways. But there are challenges for framing teaching assistants' work in the work of teachers even though they work side by side, and we will discuss these in the next section.

CHALLENGES AND POSSIBILITIES IN DESCRIBING THE WORK OF TEACHING ASSISTANTS

Our data from the questionnaires and interviews used for our research suggest that it is difficult to describe the 'typical' work of teaching assistants. We found that there is a 'core' of work most take part in, and around this a range of other work. Teaching assistants have some 'teacher-like' experiences and these experiences vary between teaching assistants from different schools, and between individuals.

Rather than attempting to consider the work of teaching assistants as uniform, it might be more useful to establish a continuum of experiences in their practice. This ranges from 'ancillary-like' work to 'teacher-like' work, and is shown in Figure 11.2.

11.2 MODEL ILLUSTRATING THE CONTINUUM OF TEACHING ASSISTANTS' PRACTICE

Teaching assistants are placed in an important role in responding to the needs of children, and applying themselves to the process of children developing in schools over time. They are neither asked to take a 'cleaning paintpots' role, nor are they asked to take on the responsibility of classroom manager. There are widely different experiences and responsibilities according to how best to support the pupils.

Two ideas taken from interviews underpinning the model of continuum are exemplified below in Models A and B.

- *Model A*: Teaching assistants are likely to take different levels of responsibility, according to their usual role in the school. For example, one teaching assistant, although not acting as a teacher, typically takes a very 'teacher-like' role in the school in which she works. Her working day does not involve supporting students in lessons. Instead she works with groups of children with particular learning needs throughout the day. Her usual role places her very much toward the right-hand side of the continuum in Figure 11.2.

- *Model B*: Teaching assistants are likely to be mobile across this continuum according to the work they are expected to perform at different points of their working day, and between working with different members of staff. For example, another teaching assistant described that while working with her head of department she might be asked to lead sections of lessons, particularly if pupils are involved in using computers. However, when working with another teacher, photocopying and administrative work will make up most of her duties. In the latter case she is taking a much more ancillary-like role, rather than the teacher-like one in the first case, illustrating a shift across this continuum within the working day.

In defining these positions, disparate views may emerge as to the position of teaching assistants in relation to this continuum. In individual cases this can mean that different members of staff view the teaching assistant differently. For instance, one teacher might ask a teaching assistant to do some photocopying, whereas another might ask the same teaching assistant to work with a small group of students on, for example, Literacy Progress Units. One recommendation which might help clarify the activities that teachers may expect from teaching assistants is for clear job descriptions (Hemsley-Brown *et al.*, 2002). This could indeed make a difference, provided that the job description remains open enough to avoid fragmentation and too detailed technical description. Another recommendation is the government's plan to assign teaching assistants to particular streams of activity in schools: supporting teaching and learning, or supporting behaviour management.

Difficulties arise when the work of teaching assistants is defined solely in relation to the work of teachers. Competence to do or not to do particular activities is a relative matter, not only to the tasks themselves, but also to the people you are working with, and the school that you are working in. We all know that in some situations we flourish whereas in others we flounder, for no apparent reason except for the rather elusive 'it was really great' or 'it wasn't right for me'. Our professional identities are tied into our being successful and happy at work, so that it is as important to have a 'good boss' to help us understand how to do the tasks required as it is to be capable of doing the tasks themselves. Thus, teaching assistants working alongside teachers, each recognising the different contribution that each makes to teaching and learning, is likely to be a productive working relationship in which both flourish, a win–win situation. A relationship predicated on functional dissection of tasks, with poor communication, is less likely to enhance pupil learning, and is in danger of stultifying the professional growth of the adults involved, too.

► ACTIVITY 11.3

Think about three things you are doing well at school. Discuss with your colleagues ways of letting people know what you are doing effectively.

STANDARDS, QUALIFICATIONS AND PERFORMANCE MANAGEMENT

Schools operate in a culture of performance management. There is pressure on pupils to achieve more highly, and to achieve more and higher qualifications, progressing where possible on to higher education. In order for this to happen, schools themselves have to pay attention to individual pupils' progress, and check whether this is in line with their predicted performance. It is unlikely that anybody would object to pupils gaining more from school, provided that these higher demands are in the pupils' individual interests. Teachers are under scrutiny to make sure that they have high expectations of all their pupils, and schools are under scrutiny to ensure that the teachers are managed well enough to enable higher standards to be achieved. Ofsted (the Office for Standards in Education) inspect and report on this system; inevitably, this combined with the publication of league tables of schools results generates competition between schools; and there are consequences for schools deemed to be failing to meet national expectations.

This system is maintained through 'benchmarking', which in the UK means standards. For all the individuals in the system there are a series of standards which must be aspired to, and attained before progression to the next level. Thus, trainee teachers must meet standards for qualified teacher status (QTS) (DfES, 2002a); newly qualified teachers must meet induction standards (DfES 2001, under review in 2003) by the end of their induction period in school; experienced teachers wanting to cross the threshold and be paid more must be assessed according to threshold standards (Hextall and Mahony, 2001); and there are standards for head teachers currently being drawn up by the National Leadership College. Within this system, a cycle of recognition, target-setting and appraisal against targets provides the framework for a coherent workforce – or that's the theory. Problems occur when this system becomes an end in itself, when the needs and aspirations of the individual pupils or teachers are sacrificed for the efficient and rigorous drive to raise performance measured against targets and checklists of criteria.

In our study, teaching assistants sometimes reported that they had been on courses that 'didn't lead anywhere'. Standards are now being drawn up for higher level teaching assistants to accredit workplace practice, and to move teaching assistants on to a progression ladder that could ultimately lead to accreditation as teachers, if that is their aim. There is at least one potential snag, and that is that academic qualifications – those acquired through universities and colleges, such as Foundation or Honours degrees – are not necessarily workplace-specific. Many teaching assistants would like professional development that leads somewhere, perhaps towards a degree. Thus it is important that these two progression ladders are flexible enough so that people can step between them as and when they want. New degree opportunities are being developed with a close eye on both the QTS standards and standards for higher level teaching assistants, and it will be very important that courses offer some form of transferable accreditation, towards a degree, or professional standards, or both.

There is another equally important dimension to qualifications being useful, alongside the access to status and recognition, and that is to do with the nature of professional learning itself. In order for a person to develop their expertise, they have to meet different situations and learn from them. The process of learning from experience is sometimes called *reflective practice* (Schon, 1983), and as we learn new working practice we move along another continuum, this time from 'novice' to 'expert'. It is not always easy to sit down and analyse situations, especially in school when time is pressured, and yet people make professional progress more rapidly when there is opportunity to do this. Universities are beginning to recognise the benefits of developing academic routes for teaching assistants that focus particularly on providing a space to engage in, and give credit for, this professional reflection on workplace activities.

Pam, who has undertaken a course for a year, puts it perfectly:

> I now understand more about what teachers are doing. Before, I was blindly following their lead, whereas now I know the pressures that are on them and I feel that I can make suggestions about how to do things, but I also see things from a pupil's point of view as the pupils talk to us more than they talk to teachers. I feel more confident as a teaching assistant because I see the teaching from the classroom, so I see things as the pupils do, rather than as the teachers do, but at the same time, I am more aware of why teachers do certain things now.

Pam is very clear about her part in the professional landscape. What she describes is the development of her practice in the context of a university qualification. For those teaching assistants we spoke to, this was the case where teachers were supportive and allowed teaching assistants to try things out in the classrooms they shared. This, together with increased confidence, were the strongest elements of professional development we found.

Your line manager should help you to develop professionally as he or she affects your conditions of work, promotion prospects, appraisal and opportunities for professional development and in-service training. Your line manager is likely to be a member of the school teaching team – perhaps a special educational needs coordinator – but may not be one of the teachers you work with. In some schools, senior teaching assistants have considerable responsibility for other, less experienced teaching assistants. What is important is the link between your line manager and the school management because if you do undertake further training you will gain immeasurably by having a supervisor or mentor to help you.

Up-to-date information on continuing professional development will be available from various help lines and websites. The first port of call might be your supervisor, local education authority, university or college or the Teacher Training Agency.

► ACTIVITY 11.4

Where are you now and what would you like further study to provide? Write a letter to yourself, and give it to someone to post to you in six months' time. In the letter, set out what qualifications you hope to achieve over what time scale, and what you need to set in place now so that your aims are achievable.

REFERENCES
■

DfES (2001a) *The Induction Period For Newly Qualified Teachers* DfES 582/2001. London: Public Enquiry Unit, and online at www.dfes.gov.uk/publications

DfES (2002a) *Qualifying to Teach: Professional Standards for Qualified Teacher Status and Requirements for Initial Teacher Training.* London: DfES/TTA, and online *http://www.canteach.gov.uk*

DfES (2002b) *Developing the Role of School Support Staff: Consultation Paper.* London: DfES, October 2002.

Eraut, M. (1994) *Developing Professional Knowledge and Competence.* London: Falmer Press.

Hemsley-Brown, J., Cunningham, M., Morton, R. and Sharp, C. (2002) *Education Decision-making Under Scrutiny: The impact of local government modernisation.* Phase 2. Slough: NFER.

Hextall, I. and Mahony, P. (2001) 'Testing, Testing: teacher assessment in England', *Teaching Education* 12 (1): 35–47.

Schon, D.A. (1983) *The Reflective Practitioner: How professionals think in action.* Cambridge, Mass: MIT Press.

Thorp, J., Robinson, C., Jacklin, A. and Drake, P. (2002) *Routes into Teaching for Teaching Assistants.* Unpublished report to the DfES: University of Sussex, July 2002.

CHAPTER 12

Moving on

If you are reading this chapter it is likely that you are thinking about, or have already made a decision about, further training. But training for what? What do you want to do next? And how will you go about this? You may be very clear about what you want to do, but be wondering about how best to achieve your goal. Alternatively, you may not be very clear about what you want to move on to next and instead be weighing up the various options available. This chapter aims to explore and clarify some of these options and possible routes so you can make a more considered and informed decision.

The sections in this chapter are as follows:

- **Introduction.**
- **Where are you now and where are you coming from?**
- **Higher-level teaching assistants.**
- **Routes into teaching.**
- **School experience.**
- **Getting where you want to go.**

INTRODUCTION

Starting to think about moving on implies you are starting from somewhere, even if you feel you are still at the starting blocks (and if you are reading this, you've definitely left them behind!). Wherever you are, you are now in a system of progression in relation to qualified professional status, whether to become a higher-level teaching assistant or a teacher. You are also at a point from which there may be several pathways and exit points. These can seem very confusing at first, but how have they come about?

A lot of work has been carried out over the years tackling questions such as: What is professional knowledge? What do people need to be able to do to qualify as a member of a profession? How competent do they need to be? How do we describe those competences? How do we assess them? (e.g. see Eraut, 1994). At first glance these may seem to be relatively obvious questions; after all, we wouldn't want a surgeon to operate on us unless they had carried out that kind of operation before and knew something about our illness, nor would we want to let loose a teacher who knew nothing about the subject they were to teach. But here lies the first problem: how much do we expect teaching assistants and teachers to know, and by when? Is it possible (and does it make sense) to separate out different kinds of professional knowledge that we should expect of teaching assistants and teachers? How much experience should they have had before they should be deemed 'competent'? How much is enough? As soon as we start to think more carefully about these sorts of questions, we begin to understand the nature of the problem.

Even if we could be clear, and agree about exactly what, and how much, knowledge people need to qualify as a member of a profession, another problem that arises is how this knowledge can be acquired. Traditional approaches to teacher education used a model based on 'theory to practice'. That is, theory of teaching and learning would be taught, usually in colleges or universities and often divorced from the professional context, and then students were expected to put that theory into practice, to apply it to the classroom. In contrast to this top-down model, an apprenticeship approach emphasises the importance of the practical knowledge of teachers and how professional knowledge can develop through immersing students in classroom experiences. More recently, there has been increasing emphasis on the importance of school-based and reflective approaches to professional development, which emphasise reflection-in-action and reflection-on-action (Furlong et al., 2000). One thing that does emerge as important is the partnership between higher-education institutions and schools and local education authorities, in the professional development of teachers.

Thus over the years differing theories and models of how best to train teachers have been developed and, within this framework, the training of higher-level teaching assistants has come about. Similar kinds of questions have been tackled: What should teaching assistants know? Are there different types of knowledge for different teaching assistant roles? How can teaching assistants best acquire this knowledge? What sort of support will they need? How should it best be organised? It is out of thinking such as this that a range of routes for the training of teaching assistants has emerged.

This in itself is complex, but there are in addition a number of other factors that influence what teaching assistants and teachers should be taught, many of which are hotly debated in schools and universities, i.e. in professional and academic contexts. During the last two decades, for instance, the emphasis of successive governments on raising standards in schools, especially in literacy and numeracy, has been influential. In order to support these developments, there have been changes in the kinds of teaching approaches that teachers are trained to use in schools, and these are reflected in what is required in the training of both teaching assistants and teachers. For example, when more literacy and numeracy were included in the curriculum for trainee primary teachers, foundation subjects (e.g. arts and humanities) were significantly reduced. There have been questions asked about whether these sorts of changes are always straightforwardly a good thing, and whether there has been a subtle 're-shaping' of what the government judges a 'good' teacher to be (e.g. Mahony and Hextall, 1998).

Deciding how 'good' a teacher may be, and whether or not they are competent enough to gain qualified teacher status (QTS) and become a member of the teaching profession, brings us to a consideration of how we assess training. Competence-based education and training has its roots in teacher education in the USA. In the UK, there has been a growing critique of the approach in relation to initial teacher education (Hustler and McIntyre,1996; Calderhead and Shorrock, 1997), especially when the complexity of school life becomes reduced to a focus on what has been called 'performativity'. Do we perhaps focus on 'performance' at the expense of, for instance, relationships within schools?

Currently in England we have a set of standards for qualified teacher status (DfES, 2002a) against which trainee teachers are assessed. We also have an emerging training framework for teaching assistants (DfES, 2002b) with, at the time of writing, a draft set of standards for higher-level teaching assistants. The latter follow the structure of the standards for qualified teacher status. This kind of model (a *standards model*) essentially creates a system where a set of objectives is identified and agreed as important or essential to the profession, in relation to which training may be developed (as we discussed above, this process is not unproblematic). Against these objectives, each individual's needs can then be identified, training planned, and progress towards attainment can be monitored, reviewed and assessed.

This kind of process of performance management is fairly widespread in state schools today with teachers (engaged in continuing professional development activities) as well as with trainee teachers and teaching assistants. However, the culture of performance management in your school, i.e. the ways in which your school engages with the process, is likely to be a very influential factor in relation to how you develop. For instance, what value does the school attach to your role and to your desire to progress? What is the nature of your targets, and how were they agreed (e.g. were they set for you or negotiated)? What kind of support do you receive? How is your progress monitored and how helpful is this (both for you and in terms of school development)? Your progress in relation to these pathways may, in part, be related to performance management in your school.

In this first section, we have looked fairly critically at the theoretical landscape and your place within it. Remember, keep thinking and keep asking questions. Part of becoming a professional is learning to think critically.

WHERE ARE YOU NOW AND WHERE ARE YOU COMING FROM?

Before you start thinking about moving on, it is a good idea to begin by thinking about where you are now and where you are coming from. In Section I of this book, we spent time reflecting on the kinds of skills and abilities you were bringing with you into higher education and the kinds of experiences that would support your development. This is a useful process to go through again at this point, although it is likely that the range of experiences you will bring with you at this stage will make this an easier and more productive process. Do also keep in mind that entry requirements to higher-education institutions may vary if you are a mature student. You will need to find this out – there is more about this at the end of the section.

PERSONAL REFLECTION

Perhaps the first thing to consider is your own personal circumstance. What is happening in your personal life? Although it could be argued that there is never a good time to return to study, it would be equally true to say that some periods in our lives may be more conducive to study than others. As we established in Chapter 2, entering and working in higher education does require some juggling of different aspects of our lives. Therefore it is a good thing to start by thinking through those aspects in the light of your experiences to date. Do you have the time and the resources? Who will support you and who will you be supporting? If you continue to study, will you still have time for yourself, your family and friends? What about your lifestyle – are there things you may have to change in order to undertake this course? Some people talk about putting aspects of their life 'on hold' while they study – will you need to do this, and if so, can you do so? There are lots of things to think through.

QUALIFICATIONS

The second thing to consider as you now take stock are your qualifi-cations. Think about which qualifications you have and list these (it is likely that you will need to do this anyway for any application you make). Go through the awards and grades you received and list them chronologi-cally (check you know the date that you received the award). It is sometimes useful to include courses you took, but perhaps didn't sit the examination; for instance, you may have taken A-level English as an evening class, but never sat the examination. Once you have your list, you then need to check that you still have all your certificates. This is important because universities and colleges usually need to see them at some point. If you have any missing, don't worry. Contact the school or college you attended or the examination board for help.

As well as formal qualifications, don't forget to think about any relevant informal 'qualifications'. For instance, you may have attended some short, unaccredited courses run by your local education authority. Make a separate list of these, too, again with dates, but this time also include length of course (e.g. a day course on the literacy strategy; one afternoon a week for one term on managing behaviour; etc.).

▊EXPERIENCE

Working as a teaching assistant in schools will have provided you with many experiences. Take time to think about the different things you have done. When you start thinking back, you may be surprised at the range. Make a note of anything that may be relevant. Now think about your experience out of school, or in previous employment. List what is relevant here. For instance, you may have trained as a swimming instructor and then run a swimming club for youngsters.

▊SKILLS, KNOWLEDGE AND CONFIDENCE

Lastly, it is a good idea to think through what relevant skills and knowledge you have and where your strengths and confidence lie. For instance, you may be a good organiser or play the piano, or maybe you have useful computer skills; any of these skills may be relevant or useful for your future career pathway.

Now is a good time to tackle Activity 12.1. This task is not meant to be definitive, but to get you thinking about where you are now and also to help you reflect on where you are coming from.

▶ACTIVITY 12.1

Taking stock: a checklist for thinking about yourself

Using Figure 12.1 as a structure, in the left-hand column list all the things that are important to you and your circumstances, and all the things that relate to your qualifications, experiences and skills. Then in the right-hand column, add any thoughts you have about each, and actions you feel you must or would like to take.

The next two sections discuss training for those wanting to become a higher-level teaching assistant or to follow a route into teaching. Depending on the career pathway you wish to take, you may wish to go straight to the relevant section, missing out the section that does not apply to you. If you are a mature student with non-standard qualifications, you will need to find out what the entry requirements are of your chosen college, university or training organisation.

For mature students, entry qualifications for courses and programmes in higher education vary considerably. For instance, in some universities for

Have you thought about?	Your thoughts and actions
Personal circumstances ● You ● Your family ● Your support network ● Your friends	
Your qualifications ● Formal qualifications ● Your certificates ● Informal qualifications	
Your experience ● In school ● Previous employment ● Family ● Out of school	
Skills, knowledge and confidence ● ● ●	
Other things to think about ● ● ●	

12.1   TAKING STOCK: A CHECKLIST FOR THINKING ABOUT YOURSELF

some degrees you would need three good grades at A-level. However, this is not necessarily the case for all degree programmes and all universities. Although higher-education institutions are concerned that they do not take students onto courses where they may struggle or fail, there is an increasing recognition that some mature students may not have traditional qualifications but may still have the potential to become good students, benefit from the programme and achieve a good standard. Some programmes of study do require certain prerequisite skills (e.g. some science degrees) and in these cases, a foundation year may well be available. Other programmes are more accessible (the reasons for this are complex, and not within the scope of this chapter). It is important to contact the institution you are thinking of applying to, and send for and read their prospectus, paying particular attention to advice for mature students. Then if you have any further questions, contact the admissions tutor at the institution and talk to them. The prospectus and details of who to contact will probably be published on the institution's website.

You will find it helpful to have your completed checklist (Figure 12.1) with you when you do this.

HIGHER-LEVEL TEACHING ASSISTANTS

What is a higher-level teaching assistant? At a common-sense level, a higher-level teaching assistant is one who works at a 'higher level' than other teaching assistants and support staff in school. However, at the time of writing, the term is being introduced by the government in relation to a new role for teaching assistants. This role will involve teaching assistants providing a more substantial contribution to teaching and learning within the classroom (under the direction of qualified teachers). Standards and a training programme are currently being developed for this role. Have a look at the following website for further details and information: www.teachernet.gov.uk/teachingassistants.

An investigation of training provision for teaching assistants, in advance of these newly proposed national developments, revealed that there is currently a range of training available. For example, in our research we found that in the southern region of England, there were three broad categories of training provision:

- short unaccredited professional development courses specifically for teaching assistants

- vocational qualifications, accredited as part of the national qualifications framework

- higher-education programmes and courses which provided training from certificate to degree level, also within the national qualifications framework.

Within these categories, although there were a variety of levels of courses, it would arguably be somewhat inaccurate to describe pathways through these courses as 'progression routes'. Teaching assistants were having to find their way through an often confusing array of courses, with the additional problem that sometimes they took accredited courses, only to find at a later date that they were not able to use these towards a qualification.

You may have found yourself in the position described above, and this is where the new government proposals for training are to be welcomed. The proposals set out three progression routes for teaching assistants as follows:

- *The pedagogical route*, which focuses on teaching and learning processes and is therefore appropriate for all teaching assistants who work predominantly supporting in classrooms.

- *The behaviour and guidance route*, which, as its name suggests, focuses mainly on professional development linked to pastoral, attendance and behavioural responsibilities of teaching assistants, particularly offering support for those teaching assistants who work with pupils who present with more challenging behaviour.

- *The administration and organisation route*, which focuses on professional development for support staff who have administrative roles in schools (for example, bursars).

It is proposed that training will provide clear progression routes from induction to higher-level status. At the time of writing, it is proposed that there may be different levels of training (post induction up to the equivalent of NVQ levels 4 or 5). As you embark on further training, the emphasis within the proposals on 'joined-up thinking' is important. Coherence and flexibility should help establish clear pathways through the routes, and a clearer sense of professionalism for the role of teaching assistants.

Please note: Because at the time of writing these proposals are being developed, it is important that you consult the government websites for up-to-date information. In addition, when you apply for a course, make sure you ask about progression in relation to the course, especially as the new routes will be linked to the standards for qualified teacher status. If in the future you would like to choose this career (see the introductory section of this chapter) it is important that any training you undertake now will help you achieve this goal.

ROUTES INTO TEACHING

There are an increasing number of routes into teaching and if this is the career you wish to follow, you will need to consider carefully which route is right for you. This will really depend on aspects such as your qualifications, skills, experiences and personal circumstances. If you have not yet read the second section of this chapter and carried out Activity 12.1, you may wish to do so before reading on, as it is important to be clear where you are now and where you are coming from, before thinking about which route into teaching may be best for you.

In England all routes into teaching are linked to the standards for qualified teacher status (DfES, 2002a). This means that whichever route you take, you will still be addressing the same set of standards as trainees following any of the other routes. It is the route itself which differs, not the outcome. As teaching is an all-graduate profession, you must have a degree to achieve qualified teacher status. Some people prefer to take a degree that is geared specifically to teaching; other people concentrate on getting their degree first and then take a postgraduate course that trains them as a teacher. The key routes can be categorised as follows.

UNDERGRADUATE ROUTE

People who follow this route usually take a BA, BEd or BSc with training for qualified teacher status built into the degree programme. The degree will combine elements in subject studies (e.g. mathematics or science), professional studies and school-based training. These programmes are generally three to four years full-time or pro-rata part-time. Look out for new programmes designed specifically for teaching assistants. Some of these new programmes have been developed as full honours degrees; others are built around the new foundation degree (see Figure 12.2).

POSTGRADUATE ROUTE

The usual postgraduate route is the Postgraduate Certificate in Education (PGCE), which is a one-year, largely school-based programme, with training being given by both higher education and school-based tutors. As the title implies, this programme is postgraduate, so you need a degree in order to access it. In addition to the one-year PGCE, some higher-education institutions now offer a flexible postgraduate route which is modular and designed more around the needs and circumstances of trainees, and may be completed in less than one full academic year.

▊ EMPLOYMENT-BASED ROUTES

These are relatively new routes into teaching which allow schools to employ people who are not yet qualified to teach. The trainee is then trained on the job through what is known as the Graduate Teacher Programme (GTP) or the Registered Teacher Programme (RTP). In the GTP, you would need to be a graduate to gain access to the programme (i.e. you would already need to have a degree) and in the RTP, you could complete your degree while training. Both of these employment-based routes tend to be for mature applicants.

These routes are illustrated diagrammatically in Figure 12.2 and there are a number of ways in which you can find out more about them. The Teacher Training Agency (TTA) and DfES websites and the staff from these departments are very helpful if you contact them for information. You will also find that schools, the local education authority as well as higher-education institutions will all be able to offer advice.

SCHOOL EXPERIENCE
▬

School experience is crucial to all training, whether for teaching assistants or trainee teachers. Thus whatever training you choose to do next, one thing that will be common to all routes will be school experience. This is where as a teaching assistant you will already have many relevant skills and experiences to build on from your work in schools. However, you may find that with some of the things you do in schools, you are so used to doing them that you now carry them out almost without consciously thinking about them. We all do this. When we learn new skills we think about them a great deal and this helps the learning process. As we get more used to them, the tasks become more automatic or routine. This means that our brains don't go into overload when a new skill comes along.

Learning in the workplace is an important aspect of professional learning. You will find that it is an integral part of all training routes – whether professional training for teaching assistants or routes into teaching. As we saw in Chapter 11, some types of professional knowledge are essentially tacit; that is, they are not easily explained to others (or to yourself). This is often because they have become so automatic or routine that it is hard for us to unpack them and really understand what we do. Learning in the workplace, rather than in isolation from it, requires you to develop skills of reflection.

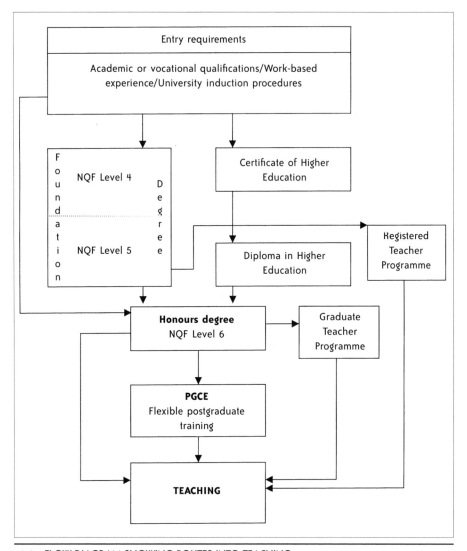

12.2   FLOW DIAGRAM SHOWING ROUTES INTO TEACHING

Note: You may come across the new National Qualifications Framework (NQF) in which undergraduate levels 1, 2 and 3 are replaced by NQF levels 4, 5 and 6 as in Figure 12.2.

Reflection can take place *in-action* (this is not as easy as you might think) or *on-action* (i.e. after the event). Because so many actions, or skilled teaching behaviours, become increasingly routinised, and knowledge becomes tacit, it is not always easy for a teaching assistant or a teacher to explain to someone what they did and why – this is where reflection comes in. A good analogy is driving a car. The skills involved in driving become increasingly and essentially routinised. For instance, if a non-driver asks you to explain what you just did as you carried out a hill start, you may not be able to explain, or indeed remember in detail all your actions. What you did was probably carried out unconsciously, the result of having routinised your driving behaviour, allowing you to concentrate on other things, such as potential hazards. If the non-driver then asked you to talk through what you are doing as you balance the clutch and accelerator to do the hill start, you will probably get it wrong, perhaps rolling back or stalling the car. When you learned to drive, your instructor will have helped you to think back over what you did and the consequences of your own actions, e.g. dissecting your own hill start.

In the classroom, in order to make explicit your growing professional knowledge and understandings, you will be required to reflect on your own experiences. This will include teaching and learning behaviours you have observed as well as your own actions. This reflection-on-action will be important in helping you to learn from your school experiences. It is highly likely that you will be asked to keep a portfolio to record your reflections. In time, you will find your ability to reflect-in-action will increase.

One thing to keep in mind is that it is not the school experience itself, but your learning from this experience that is important. Two people may have the same school experiences, but one may learn far more from them than the other. Developing skills of reflection, making your learning explicit, are very important skills that will help you develop as a professional.

GETTING WHERE YOU WANT TO GO

By now you probably have a clearer idea of where you want to go. Having a picture of the professional landscape before you start is helpful, but now you need to get down to planning your route in more detail. First things first: check that you have your general direction clear and you know what you want to move on to do. This may be a long-term goal (become a higher-level teaching assistant or a teacher) or it may be a shorter-term goal (you may want to do some short accredited courses to increase your understanding of an area of your work and to 'test the water' in terms of further study).

Once your goal is clear, you need to be sure you know what route to take to achieve it. Make sure you ask lots of questions and really be sure you are signing on for the right course for you. For instance, what level are your accredited courses? What can you do with the credits afterwards? Is there a progression route available if 'testing the water' proves positive?

Once your goal and your route are clear, check your resources. Take stock. Have you thought through your support structure (see Activity 12.1)? Will this sustain you while you study? In school, will you have the support of colleagues? Check finances and make enquires about fees, grants and loans. Contact your school, your local education authority and the institution to which you will be applying. Keep asking questions!

As you plan your route, remember that you need to keep two things in mind – your long-term goal (e.g. to become a higher-level teaching assistant or a teacher) and your immediate or short-term goal (i.e. what you intend to do now). You need to plot the long-term route but identify and plan the smaller steps that will get you there. Once you have done that, you are ready to go. Enjoy yourself!

REFERENCES

Calderhead, J. and Shorrock, S. (1997) *Understanding Teacher Education: Case studies in the professional development of beginning teachers.* London: Falmer.

DfES (2002a) *Qualifying to Teach: Professional Standards for Qualified Teacher Status and Requirements for Initial Teacher Training.* London: DfES/TTA.

DfES (2002b) *Developing the Role of School Support Staff: Consultation Paper.* London: DFES, October 2002.

Eraut, M. (1994) *Developing Professional Knowledge and Competence.* London: Falmer Press.

Furlong, J., Barton, L., Miles, S., Whiting, S. and Whitty, G. (2000) *Teacher Education in Transition: Re-forming professionalism?* Buckingham: Open University Press.

Hargreaves, A. and Fullan, M. (1992) *Understanding Teacher Development.* London: Cassell.

Hustler, D. and McIntyre, D. (1996) *Developing Competent Teachers: Approaches to professional competence in teacher education.* London: Fulton.

Mahony, P. and Hextall, I. (1998) 'Social justice and the reconstruction of teaching', *Journal of Education Policy*, 13 (4): 545–58.

References

Ayers, H., Clarke, D. and Murray, A. (2000) *Perspectives on Behaviour: a practical guide to effective interventions for teachers*, 2nd edn. London: David Fulton. (1st edn, 1995).

Bentley, T. (1998) *Learning beyond the Classroom: Education for a changing world.* London: Routledge.

Board of Education (1937) *Handbook of Suggestions for the Consideration of Teachers and Others Concerned in the Work of Public Elementary Schools.* London: HMSO.

Booth, T, Ainscow, M., Black-Hawkins, K., Vaughan, M. and Shaw, L. (2002) *Index for Inclusion: Developing learning and participation in schools*, 2nd edn. Bristol: CSIE. (1st edn, 2000).

Calderhead, J. and Shorrock, S. (1997) *Understanding Teacher Education: Case studies in the professional development of beginning teachers.* London: Falmer.

Chitty, C. and Dunford, J. (1999) *State Schools – New Labour and the Conservative Legacy.* Woburn: Woburn Press.

Cooper, B. and Dunne, M. (1999) *Assessing Children's Mathematical Knowledge: Social class, sex and problem-solving.* Buckingham: Open University Press.

Cooper, P., Smith, C.J. and Upton, G. (1994) *Emotional Behaviour Difficulties, Theory to Practice.* London: Routledge.

Cowley, S. (2001) *Getting the Buggers to Behave.* London: Continuum.

De Fazio, T. (2002) *Studying Part-time Without Stress.* Crows Nest, NSW: Allen & Unwin.

DES (1978) *Special Educational Need* (Report of the Warnock Committee). London: HMSO.

DFE (1994) *Code of Practice on the Identification and Assessment of Special Educational Needs.* London: HMSO.

DfEE/QCA (1999) *The National Curriculum (England)*. London: HMSO, and online at http://www.nc.uk.org

DfES (2001a) *The Induction Period For Newly Qualified Teachers*. DfES 582/2001 Public Enquiry Unit, and online at www.dfes.gov.uk/publications

DfES (2001b) *Youth Cohort Study: The activities and experiences of 19-year-olds: England and Wales 2000 Reference ID SFR43/2001*. London: DfES

DfES (2002a) *Qualifying to Teach: Professional Standards for Qualified Teacher Status and Requirements for Initial Teacher Training*. London: DfES/TTA, and online at http://www.canteach.gov.uk

DfES (2002b) *Developing the Role of School Support Staff: Consultation Paper*. London: DfES, October 2002.

Dolton, P. and Vignoles A. (1999) *The Labour Market Returns to Different Types of Secondary School Curricula*. Paper presented at the Royal Economic Society's 1999 Annual Conference at the University of Nottingham.

Epstein, J.L. (1995) 'School/family/community partnerships: Caring for the children we share', *Phi Delta Kappan*, 76 (9): 701–11.

Eraut, M. (1994) *Developing Professional Knowledge and Competence*. London: Falmer Press.

Furlong, J., Barton, L., Miles, S., Whiting, S. and Whitty, G. (2000) *Teacher Education in Transition: Re-forming Professionalism?* Buckingham: Open University Press.

Hallgarten, J. (2000) *Parents Exist, OK!? Issues and visions for parent-school relationships*. Southampton: IPPR.

Hargreaves, A. and Fullan, M. (1992) *Understanding Teacher Development*. London: Cassell.

Hegarty, S. and Pocklington, K. with Lucas, D. (1981) *Educating Pupils with Special Needs in the Ordinary School*. Windsor: NFER-Nelson.

Hemsley-Brown, J., Cunningham, M., Morton, R. and Sharp, C. (2002) *Education Decision-making Under Scrutiny: the impact of local government modernisation, phase 2*. Slough: NFER.

Hextall, I. and Mahony, P. (2001) 'Testing, Testing: teacher assessment in England', *Teaching Education* 12 (1): 35–47.

HMI (1959) *Primary Education: Suggestions for the consideration of teachers and others concerned with the work of primary schools*. London: HMSO.

Hustler, D. and McIntyre, D. (1996) *Developing Competent Teachers: Approaches to professional competence in teacher education.* London: Fulton.

Jacklin, A. (1996) *The Transfer Process Between Special and Mainstream Schools.* Unpublished D.Phil Thesis: University of Sussex.

Jackson, S. (1969) *Special Education in England and Wales,* 2nd edn. London: Oxford University Press. (1st edn, 1966).

Klenowski, V. (2002) *Developing Portfolios for Learning and Assessment: Processes and Principles.* London: Routledge Falmer.

Kyriacou, C. (1997) *Effective Teaching in Schools: Theory and practice,* 2nd edn. Cheltenham: Stanley Thornes. (1st edn, 1986).

MacBeath, J. and Gray, D. (2001) 'Lochgelly North Special School'. In Maden, M. (ed.) *Success Against the Odds – Five Years On: Revisiting effective Schools in disadvantaged areas.* London: Routledge Falmer.

MacPherson of Cluny, Sir W., advised by Cook, T., Sentamu, J. and Stone, R. (1999) *The Stephen Lawrence Inquiry.* Report of an inquiry presented to Parliament by the Secretary of State for the Home Department. London: The Stationery Office: February 1999.

McNamara, S. and Moreton, G. (2001) *Changing Behaviour: Teaching children with emotional and behavioural difficulties in primary and secondary classrooms,* 2nd edn. London: David Fulton. (1st edn, 1995).

Mahony, P. and Hextall, I. (1998) 'Social justice and the reconstruction of teaching', *Journal of Education Policy,* 13 (4): 545–58.

Mannion, G., Allan, J. and Nixon, J. (2000) *Finding Local Prospects in a National Prospectus: Frameworks for thinking about educational purposes. Evaluating new community schools.* University of Sterling.

NCES (1995) *Literacy, Economy and Society: Results from the International Adult Literacy Survey.* National Center for Education Statistics: Washington.

National Assembly for Wales/ACCAC (2000) *The National Curriculum in Wales.* Cardiff: ACCAC, and online at http://www.accac.org.uk.

Prosser, M. and Trigwell, K. (1999) *Understanding Learning and Teaching: The experience in higher education.* Buckingham: Society for Research into Higher Education, with Open University Press.

Rogers, B. (2000) *Behaviour Management: a whole school approach.* London: Paul Chapman.

Schon, D.A. (1983) *The Reflective Practitioner: How professionals think in action.* Cambridge, Mass: MIT Press.

Thorp, J., Robinson, C., Jacklin, A. and Drake, P. (2002) *Routes into Teaching for Teaching Assistants.* Unpublished report to the DfES: University of Sussex: July 2002.

Torrance, H. (2002) *Can Testing Really Raise Educational Standards?* Professorial Lecture 11 June 2002: University of Sussex.

Turner, J. (2002) *How to Study: a short introduction.* London: Sage.

Vincent, C. and Tomlinson, S. (1997) 'Home school relationships: the swarming of disciplinary mechanisms?', *British Educational Research Journal,* 23 (3): 361–77.

Index